Dance and politics

Manchester University Press

Dance and politics

Moving beyond boundaries

Dana Mills

Manchester University Press

Published by Manchester University Press
Altrincham Street, Manchester M1 7JA
www.manchesteruniversitypress.co.uk

British Library Cataloguing-in-Publication Data
A catalogue record for this book is available from the British Library

Library of Congress Cataloging-in-Publication Data applied for

ISBN 978 1 5261 0514 1   hardback
ISBN 978 1 5261 0515 8   paperback

First published 2017

The publisher has no responsibility for the persistence or accuracy of URLs for any external or third-party internet websites referred to in this book, and does not guarantee that any content on such websites is, or will remain, accurate or appropriate.

Typeset in Minion by Out of House Publishing

In song and dance man expresses himself as a member of a higher community: he has forgotten how to walk and speak and is on the way forward flying into the air, dancing.

Friedrich Nietzsche

You have to love dancing to stick to it. It gives you nothing back, no manuscripts to store away, no paintings to show on walls and maybe hang in museums, no poems to be printed and sold, nothing but that single fleeting moment when you feel alive.

Merce Cunningham

For my father, Harold Mills, who taught me how to love dance, books
and the world.

With love and thanks, always.

Contents

Acknowledgements

I thank everyone at Manchester University Press. I thank Chris Goto-Jones and Cissie Fu for having faith in this project since its inception. Special thanks to Caroline Wintersgill, who really made this project possible on so many levels.

I am indebted to Michael Freeden, who encouraged me to pursue this project and commented on many drafts since its inception. I thank David Leopold for his wonderful conversation on political theory and beyond, who with exceptional generosity and kindness has helped me bring many of the ideas here into writing. David's engagement with political theory has been a constant source of inspiration for me. I thank Marc Stears and Beverley Clack for their comments on an early version of this book, and for their ongoing generosity and inspiration.

I would especially like to thank practitioners who made time for me and shared their experiences of working on the various pieces I write about in the book. Lori Belilove, artistic director of the Isadora Duncan Dance Company, invited me to watch a rehearsal and spoke with me about her dance education. I spent some valuable time in the Martha Graham archives in the Library of Congress as well as in the Graham School in New York. I would particularly like to thank Janet Eilber, artistic director of the Graham Dance Company, for talking with me and giving me insights into the company's work during its time at Jacob's Pillow Dance Festival. A very special thank you goes to the inimitable Marni Thomas Wood; first, for an inspirational Graham class I carry in my body still, and then for ongoing conversations in New York and Oxford, which taught me I can never really know enough about Martha Graham. Norton Owen, director of preservation at Jacob's Pillow, made my stay there transformative and helped me through the many Graham materials the Pillow holds. Arkadi Zaides was very generous in sharing his work with me and talking with me about it.

I have benefited hugely from conversations with many scholars who engage with themes explored in this book in various ways. I would like to thank: Davide Panagia (for the best reading recommendations and for his inspiring energy), Vicki Thoms, Susan Jones, Fiona Macintosh and everyone at the APGRD, Pamela Sue Anderson (for fantastic feminist support and wonderful conversations on feminist philosophy and life beyond it), my dear friend Jonna Patterson (my favourite Rancière interlocutor who always pushes me to think further and harder), participants of an APSA panel in 2013 in which I gave an earlier version of Chapter 3 of this book, Elisabeth Anker (for support and inspiration) and my select group of theorist friends and comrades – Eloise Harding, Or Rosenboim and Genia Ivanova – for friendship, encouragement and always stimulating conversation.

I was fortunate to spend time in the classics and political science departments at Northwestern University. I thank all members of those departments, who were such hospitable hosts. Sara Monoson had made the experience happen and has been a wonderfully generous mentor to me since. I thank Mary Dietz for an inspirational exchange that has inspired me to extend my thinking what I am doing. I thank Bonnie Honig for ongoing conversations which never cease to galvanise and inspire me. Bonnie's example has been truly transformative for me.

I met Rachel Holmes too late in this project for her to suffer its full consequences. However, her never-ending passion and commitment to both social justice and writing, and her inimitable combination of principle and compassion, have been transformative for me. I thank Rachel – Sister Comrade – for her inspiration and generosity, in conversation between living and dead feminists that is always going ahead.

I have been humbled by sharing an intellectual space with one of the most powerful voices of our time on social justice, Baroness Helena Kennedy QC. Helena's uncompromising ethics have galvanised and profoundly inspired me. I will not attempt to add to the high praise that Helena receives in every possible medium of communication, but those who are blessed to know her in person will testify that she is far better than any superlatives and honours bestowed upon her. Helena is my role model in everything that is good and just in the world, and through her example always pushes me to be a better person. I thank and love Helena for being a never-ending source of inspiration for me in her extraordinary mentorship and friendship.

This book was written during my time teaching political theory at Hertford College, Oxford. I thank my colleagues for thought-provoking conversations and for support and encouragement. A special tribute goes to the very singular Principal of Hertford, Will Hutton, who makes the college a truly egalitarian, vibrant and energetic space for radical discussion about politics and justice. Will's leadership makes the college a really wonderful place to think and write in. I thank Will for his example, generosity and inspiration, for being a role model for us all in how good we can be.

A big thank you goes to my most constant interlocutors in political theory, my students, who always push me to think harder and keep my mind alive; and a special tribute goes to the women's studies MSt cohort of 2014–15 for asking me the best questions about the manuscript in the course of writing it and inspiring me in our joint effort to smash the patriarchy.

The manuscript has benefited hugely from Clare Joyce's and Kiley Hunkler's very careful reading. I cannot thank both of these brilliant women enough for their incredibly helpful comments and for being such wonderful interlocutors with me in the process of tying up this project.

I have been blessed by a fantastic posse of extraordinary friends around the world who I wish to thank: Yonatan Bar On, for cooking for me, supporting and inspiring me for so long; my gorgeous Lee Peled, whose willpower and good judgement have sustained me since our days dancing together through both personal and professional changes, and whose presence in my life is a constant mainstay of inspiration; Adi Shoham, who has shared the ride with me in so many ways and always has been there for me; my dearest Tamara Sharon-Ross, who, despite being on the other side of the Atlantic, makes my life much more worth living through her friendship; the one and only Hodaya Jane Slutsky Kashtan, for strength and inspiration over such a long time; Nancy Eisenhower and Jan Calamita, who have given me a home away from home, many fabulous conversations and the best company I could ask for in Oxford; Jane Buswell, woman of great compassion and fierce personality, for everything; Clio Kennedy-Hutchison for feminist fabulousness; and last but definitely not least, the wonderful Dawn Berry, who has made Oxford worthwhile.

My family has tolerated and supported me in the long period of working on this project. I would like to thank my sister Susan Lucas for love and support and my cousins all around the world. I would especially like to thank Julian and Margaret Haines, Louise and Matt Dunstan and Samantha and David Haines, for giving me a home in Wales.

My beloved aunt Tirza Posner has been a pillar of strength throughout my life and a ceaseless source of support and love. My mother, Gabriella Mills, has been a constant role model for me in her love of books and of the world beyond them and in always being relentlessly compassionate. My father, Harold Mills, is always my hero and the biggest inspiration on my life. This book is for him.

Introduction

Our political world is in constant motion. Our lives are continually shifting. Collective communicative structures which have held us together in various forms of communal life are relentlessly being challenged by new languages. Practices that have bound human beings together for thousands of years are transformed, gain new meaning and receive renewed significance. This book is a study of one such practice, dance.

The book intervenes in critical conjunctures in political theory, bringing together new reflections on the moving body, spaces of action and our interpretation of politics and political theory more broadly. Jodi Dean's careful examination of the Occupy movement in *The Communist Horizon*, in which, quite literally, bodies intervened in public spaces in order to reconsider distributive justice; Jane Bennett's crucial intervention into the humanist and language-driven world of political theory, *Vibrant Matter*; and Diana Coole and Samantha Frost's edited collection *New Materialisms* opened up a vista for scholars and theorists seeking new ways to consider the body in its relationship to the physical world it inhabits, as well as to understanding politics through the long-standing humanistic tradition in philosophy. However, the inspiration and galvanising force for embarking on my own argument comes from a question raised by Bonnie Honig in her reading of *Antigone*, which converses with numerous other readings of this play, from Hegel to Butler through Lacan, in her *Antigone, Interrupted*; she revisits an invitation to leave grief behind, dance all night and join the feast of Dionysus (Honig 2013: 119). Honig asks us to reconsider that invitation from the chorus; I follow her in reconsidering this invitation and yet show throughout the book that dance has served many people around the world for various purposes; it was never merely just a way to forget.

This book illuminates the power of dance to bring people together, as well as to separate them, in different moments in time as well as in different geographical and cultural locations. Throughout the book I argue that dance is a sustained method of communication that includes grammatical structures and units, just like verbal language; at the same time it is a method of intervention that brings new speaking beings into shared spaces. Dance has its own methods of interpreting values through symbolic structures. Thus dance provides interpretations of questions regarding human beings' political lives within its own system of signification. At times, these interpretations through movement challenge and transcend conceptual interpretations articulated in verbal language. Consequently, I read dance as an embodied method of communication which is a subversive practice. It challenges women's and men's perceptions of themselves as members of communities as well as their shared spaces and communal lives. Dance inserts new voices into existing communities; those voices are articulated through moving bodies.

Dance has been always been an essential part of human life. It has always occupied a central position in the manifold forms of shared human existence. Throughout time and space, women and men have expressed themselves through their moving bodies by dancing on stage, which, in turn, has moved other bodies, those of their audiences. Further, the bodies which have been moved have not kept still themselves; they have, in turn, affected other bodies and altered the way they have been perceived. Those bodies are, in and of themselves, political bodies. They are part of engrained symbolic webs that mould them and enable them to become what they are. Hence, dance and politics are always already intertwined. Dancing bodies affect bodies in the audience; all of those bodies are political entities.

Understanding dance as including linguistic and communicative features within it, as being part of a whole world, allows the study to expand into understanding issues and ideas articulated through moving bodies. In this book I show that dance indeed allowed moments of transgression and emancipation; but dance has also been used by oppressors and at times has darker sides to it than meet the eye. Thus the book draws away from the absolute alignment of the normative and emotive content that can be articulated in dance. Dance can be used to better and worsen human beings' lives. Dance can articulate joy and pain, anger and jubilation. The conceptual focus in the book is on moments in which dance has been used by moving subjects for the better. The first chapter shows the underlying conceptual logic for this focus; drawing on an assumption of equality allows me to argue that human beings utilised their bodies when they were deemed unequal and achieved greater visibility within their communities. The concluding chapter of the book will push this thesis further, into the boundaries between ethics and politics, by examining this moment of subversion through the body operating within the normative-theoretical idea of radical hope; a new ontology that gives its subject the possibility to dance a world in becoming.

It is crucial to pause here and illuminate my use of the term 'world'. The use of the term world does not correspond to a known ontological space from the so-called 'canon' of Western political thought. The argument starts from an awareness that what has been termed a 'known' world in political theory will tend to lapse into a white, middle-class, male, Judeo-Christian world. My use of the term 'world' aims to do the opposite – to look at diverse subjects who have mobilised their bodies to create systems of signification out of their own environment. Thus the book starts from the recognition that human beings occupy separate worlds which yield different meanings and forms of life.

The first chapter of the book outlines the conceptual structure as well as the arc of the argument. The argument is structured as a three-dimensional argument that occupies a space of its own; it works within the space demarcated by its axes. This is never a metaphorical space, as the argument arises from the bodies of people who danced and from the stages upon which performances took place. The book does not only consider dance for the theatre; thus the use of the term 'stage' is representative of a space allowing for communication between two bodies: one audience member and one dancer.

The first of the three axes around which the argument is structured is the tension between contraction and release – the politics inscribed within the body itself as a space, and the politics generated from interaction between two moving bodies. The second axis is the distinction between the weak reading of political dance – the representation through moving bodies of ideas previously articulated in words – and the strong reading of political dance – the creation of a phenomenologically independent world which includes its own system of inscription and world of reception. The third axis is that of sic-sensuous. The concept of sic-sensuous looks at processes of intervention occurring between two sensed and sensing bodies, when meaning is transferred and sometimes creates new methods of embodied interpretation. I turn away from those narrating the story of the politics of dance – theorists and historians – towards the dancers and audience members themselves. I ask that we, as readers–spectators of the argument, become more attentive to the dancing bodies that have interrupted and transfigured our symbolic frameworks across space and time. I have constructed my conceptual framework from a choreographic, critical reading of Jacques Rancière's concept of dissensus. Rancière sees the essence of politics 'as the manifestation of dissensus as the presence of two worlds in one' (Rancière 2010: 37). Dissensus is the collision of two worlds, one intervening in the other and reconfiguring what we understand as political life. Those moments of dissensus are moments in which webs of sensations are reconfigured and people who have been deemed unequal show that they are equal speaking beings. Elsewhere Rancière reads dissensus as a conflict between sensory presentation and the way of making sense of this presentation. Inequality for Rancière is not an ontological condition but rather a presupposition that only functions when it is put into action (Rancière 2009). Following Rancière, I cast the conceptual limelight on moments in which dance enables embodied enunciations to be perceived and received as equal to verbal language. In that moment of intervention dance interrupts those systems of signification that marginalise dancers and their audiences.

At the same time, many of Rancière's interlocutors and commentators have noted the problematics of understanding politics as interruption for our understanding of political space. Swyngedouw writes: 'the "people" do not pre-exist the political sequence through which it is called into being as a procedure of living-in-common (sic) … It is this lack of foundation, the gaping whole (the void) in the social that renders its founding impossible and that inaugurates the political' (Swyngedouw 2011: 376). Lois McNay argues that Rancière's reading of politics is anti-ontological (McNay 2014). Bosteels writes: 'the whole purpose of reasoning in terms of such a gap or a distance … lies in the capacity of a political subject to find a foothold in the void so as to move beyond, instead of merely denouncing an otherwise worthwhile undeniable lack of legitimacy revealed in this distance' (Bosteels 2003: 132). Dikec notes that 'for Rancière politics is all about creating spaces where a wrong can be addressed and equality can be demonstrated; re-configuring, in other words, the distribution of the sensible by staging equality, seeking a new distribution that does not deny this equality' (Dikec 2005: 674). Rancière yields a paradoxical reading of politics as redistributing space but lacking a space of its own, within which we try to find spaces for subjects to legitimise themselves as speaking beings while dissenting against wrongs that marginalise them. Moreover, the effort to engage Rancière's conception of dissensus within embodied practices shows the ontological contradictions within his work. Drawing upon Rancière's discussion of redistribution of the sensible as enabling new modes of appearance is appealing to those seeking to interpret embodied practices. Nibbelink makes this

astute comment: 'Rancière's distribution of the sensible hardly pays attention to the possibility of corporeal intelligence: knowledge that is present
in affects and sensations' (Nibbelink 2012: 418). Whereas Rancière asks
us to focus upon the reorganisation of the sensible, knowledge conveyed
through the sensed body, the actual body as the thinking and sensed
organism of perception par excellence has very little conceptual room in
this framework. Thus I shift the theoretical focus away from the ontological critiques outlined above.

This shift towards listening to the body is grounded in the understanding that the moving body, the flesh that learns and teaches to be mobilised and shifted, is never without weight and never without ontology.
My reconfiguration of Rancière's dissensus – together with his normative
underpinnings – insists on the equality of human beings, even when this
equality is not recognised in other formations or configurations. At the
same time, my interpretation asks us to be more attentive to voices raised
by moving bodies. I focus the first chapter of the book on the analytic-
conceptual framework that generates the concept of sic-sensuous, which
focuses on the sensed body and its potential to interrupt shared worlds.

This book is motivated by one central question: how can we expand
our notion of what is political so that it includes dance? This question
in turn is teased out into three intimately related questions: firstly, how
can we expand who we consider parts of our political communities?
Secondly, what do we consider a political enunciation? And thirdly, who
do we consider a speaking subject? Accordingly, I ask four related questions: is dance seen as a legitimate avenue to express politics? When does
politics occur in dance? Why does politics occur in dance? What conception of political dance does this interchange yield? Those questions will
reappear throughout the book in various guises as they provided me with
the theoretical as well as the political motivation for this investigation.
Dance, I argue, has always been part of human beings' lives, though it
has not always been understood as a legitimate way to articulate their
political self. It is in situations in which human beings started being considered as part of the community through their use of dance that I see the
moment of politics in dance happening. This book explores moments in
which people contest their marginal positioning through the use of their
bodies.

This book focuses on moments in which those moving bodies have
altered the way human beings have perceived themselves through
other modes of communication. Thus this book carries a doubly critical message. It radicalises the way politics is perceived, away from formal institutions towards dance as a practice central to human lives

around the globe. At the same time, it probes into various political functions that dance carries which are not always elaborated within choreographic studies. The book asks us to reconsider what we perceive as political dance; and in this process to ask questions about definitions of both components of this concept – politics and dance. Throughout the book political theorists, choreographers, politicians, dance scholars, legal theorists, cultural theorists and philosophers will make entrances and exits into the conversation from its conceptual wings. They will be hovering at the margins of the text, asking to expand the discussion beyond disciplinary boundaries and across various realms in which human beings act as political and choreographic beings.

The book employs a triadic argument. First, it argues that dance is interruptive to politics enunciated in other symbolic structures – in particular, words – in that it shows the equality of the dancing subjects to speaking subjects even when this equality is not articulated elsewhere.

Second, this book argues that dance is a method of inscription; a system of communication that has a multiplicity of characteristics and allows its subjects to speak with their bodies. Thus by interrupting politics articulated in words, dancing subjects also affirm and develop their embodied methods of inscription.

Third, dance creates shared embodied spaces: between dance makers and dancers; between dancers among themselves; and between dancers and spectators. Those shared spaces are created by dance as a method of inscription; dance, in its communicative power, allows for people to share spaces in their bodies and provides choreographic characteristics that allow those spaces to unravel. In those shared spaces bodies communicating with each other are equal; when one body inscribes upon another it affirms the underlying equality that allows for this moment of sharing to arise. At the same time those moments of sharing also elucidate the differences between the bodies which partake in this visceral communication.

The argument aims especially to shed light on moments in which it is hard to create shared spaces in other methods of communication; when dance transcends other systems of signification that render some bodies privileged and others inferior.

The argument proceeds as follows. The first chapter presents the conceptual framework and the theoretical backdrop underlying the argument of the book. In this chapter I examine the assumptions and methods employed in the book in their intellectual context and problematise the conceptual structure of the argument. The first chapter sets the argument of the book in the context of dance studies and the political theory from which this book draws.

The second chapter focuses on the work of dance pioneer Isadora Duncan. Isadora Duncan contested the hegemony of ballet as she argued that it did not express her subjective being. In her choreographic intervention Duncan affirmed the independent power of dance as a method of expression. The chapter argues that she legitimated herself as a speaking being and her system of movement as a method of inscription. The chapter focuses on moments of contradiction between Duncan's turbulent association with politics articulated in words and her re-articulation of dance as an independent system of inscription. It investigates the shared spaces she created in her intervention and the tensions they created with her politics as articulated in words.

The third chapter focuses on the work of Martha Graham. Graham responded to Duncan's intervention in modern dance. She had complex relationships with the politics of her time. She created a different system of inscription which created different unique opportunities for shared spaces. Whereas her political goals, articulated in words, claimed that her body can create shared universal spaces, her system of inscription allows for contradictions in her dancers' and spectators' embodied being to be performed. I show one such moment of intervention in which her system of inscription created a subversive moment in performance against the backdrop of the Cold War.

The fourth chapter looks at the communicative power of dance in political circumstances in which some subjects are not allowed to use words. I examine the gumboot dance tradition in South Africa; this arose out of the mining industry, in which the miners were not allowed to converse, and hence they developed a system of movement to communicate messages. The chapter shows how the method of inscription elaborated in gumboot dance created moments for embodied sharing between the miners when the legal and political frameworks of that time did not allow other forms of communication and sharing to occur. I show the contradictions between the subversive potential that gumboot dance entailed for its subjects and instances of the use of the dance to reaffirm the racial and economic inequality that created the conditions in which the dance developed.

The fifth chapter discusses One Billion Rising, a global movement founded by Eve Ensler that uses dance to protest against violence against women, to protest against the legal and political marginalisation of survivors of sexual violence, and to create a connection between the impact of violence on women's bodies and their reappropriation of public spaces through the flash mob. I discuss the tension between the aim to create a universal shared space for subjects to reclaim their bodies and the response of individual bodies, grounded in specific political embodied languages, to that goal.

The sixth and final chapter discusses the relationship between dance and human rights. Throughout the book I show that dance has transcended the geopolitical boundaries agreed upon in verbal language. In this chapter I argue that by affirming universal equality of all speaking subjects, dance can allow us to assert the idea and ethos of the human rights regime. Using two case studies from Palestine and Israel I argue that dance is a way to affirm belonging to the human rights regime from below through embodied methods of inscription. I investigate the dabke, Palestine's national dance, which has created a shared space with a unique system of inscription allowing for shared Palestinian identity as well as singular languages to be articulated in motion. I also investigate an Israeli dance work which allows Palestinian subjects to protest human rights abuse without speaking on their behalf. I argue that the use of dance as a system of inscription in these two case studies allows for human rights claims to be made by subjects in circumstances in which legal-political mechanisms hinder articulation of those claims. I show that dance is a method of claiming human rights locally, through a dialogue between two moving bodies, and at the same time affirming the universal idea underlying the human rights regime, equality in dignity of relationships between subjects.

I then proceed to the book's conclusions, which draw on the sun dance, a dance performed by the Crow people, a Native American tribe. I argue that dance can offer a world-in-becoming; it builds shared worlds where they do not yet exist.

A note on method

The main aim of the book is to highlight injustices and to show ways in which dance has attempted to combat them, either by illuminating the language developed by the dancer against their oppressor in a singular instance or to highlight injustice beyond that instance. This book starts from an honest effort to take more seriously – and to listen to – dancers' embodied voices. It is a quest to reincorporate them into our contemporary political discourse. Therefore, the book draws upon a few methodological standpoints which are intertwined in the argument.

First, the book tries to find instances in which dance goes beyond a delimited, defined audience. It seeks to trace moments in which dance has also gone beyond its boundaries in the physical sense – beyond the boundaries of the physical space to which it was assigned. At the same time, the process of writing this book is doing exactly that – extending the scope of influence of dance beyond its more traditional areas of discourse. Therefore, whereas I have researched the danced examples discussed in many different sources – live performances, archives, interviews with dancers and choreographers – every danced instant I discuss is supported by a YouTube clip which the reader can easily access. My effort is to elucidate egalitarianism within dance; to do so, I am utilising resources that are doing exactly that.

Second, the case studies of the book vary widely. Isadora Duncan and Martha Graham are two of the most researched women in the history of twentieth-century dance. On the other hand, there is no substantial writing as yet about the One Billion Rising movement. There has been some anthropological research on dabke and gumboot dance, but no specifically political readings of these instances of political dance. Thus the chapters vary in the sources they draw upon. At the same time, I sustain the same chapter structure throughout the book: political dance through words, close readings of the choreographic works and a discussion of their reception. This is not only a methodological but an ethical point. My danced interlocutors occupy an equal position for my conversation, whether they have been subjects of multiple books or whether this is the first discourse to engage their movement.

Third, for the analysis in the book I draw on diverse experiences and dancing voices. My position towards all discourses is that of a spectator who is experiencing the pieces from the outside; at the same time I am bringing to light the dancers' voices themselves, speaking from inside their danced world. I place the reader in the space of the spectator of these diverse performances. The book is always sensitive to the conditions of production and performances of various dances, and, indeed, dwells upon some moments of cultural appropriation and silencing of voices by hegemonic discourses. Thus I invite the reader to view the performances I discuss in multiple theatres, to which they are invited through the argument.

Fourth, I use the concepts of performer and dancer throughout the book when analysing dance. This does not imply reducing dance to theatrical dance. I use these concepts to draw attention to the dialogical nature of dance, which is always relational, always aimed towards an Other.

The book's argument spills from the singular dancing body towards the shared space it creates in its method of inscription. In order to elucidate this process many sources and points of view are discussed: dancers, spectators, politicians, policy makers, theorists and philosophers. The book uses reviews, interviews, theoretical works, commentaries and close readings of chorography. I aid the reader in shifting points of view and experiencing the manifold perspectives that constitute dance as a world.

Lastly, this book is a feminist text, whether it explicitly problematises questions of gender (as in Chapters 2, 3 and 5) or not. The book starts from the quest to redeem danced voices considered unequal and outside the public sphere; and from the awareness that those voices were quite often mobilised by women. The Cartesian mind/body divide which sees the female body as the 'other' of male rationality is constantly being questioned and unsettled throughout the argument. Bringing women's bodies onto centre stage – as equal interlocutors to male politicians and theorists – is not only a methodological act but a normative choice.

At the same time, the book starts from the awareness that there is a myriad of deep cleavages and divides to be overcome when writing about – and acting for – social justice in the name of equality. Gumboot dancers exploited by white bosses in South Africa; Palestinian dabke dancers undergoing daily human rights abuses at Israeli checkpoints; all these examples (which are more exemplars than examples) are inextricably linked to the feminist ethos of listening to voices deemed marginal. I illuminate phenomenological worlds of subjects seen as unequal, worlds that would not intersect, coincide or touch those who see them as inferior;[1] however, I show that those worlds can come into an embodied unique dialogue through the power of dance. Demarcations placed in words are transcended when two worlds clash and new communities are founded. Those communities are founded in multifarious interpretations of the power that dance gives human beings, wherever they are and whenever they dance – the multitude of moments of passion and commitment, dedication and, more than anything, life in movement.

Note

1   I draw my ontology and epistemology directly from Eleanor Marx's 'The Woman Question from a Socialist Point of View' (1886) in which she writes: 'the life of woman does not coincide with that of man. Their lives do not intersect; in many cases do not even touch. Hence the life of the race is stunted.' In my methodology I examine many other worlds that, following Marx's intervention, still do not intersect and do not touch and leave our race stunted more than a hundred years since the publication of this foundational text. My reading is indebted in full to Rachel Holmes's radical rereading and re-examination of Marx's work and its significance for the twenty-first century (Holmes 2014).

1

Moving beyond boundaries: writing on the body

The book is written by many bodies who danced and inscribed their worlds upon the intersections between dance and politics. The argument is a three-dimensional space bounded by three axes; in this chapter I elaborate, explore and problematise the three axes which demarcate the space of the argument. The ontology upon which the argument acts is twofold. On the one hand the argument is grounded in the dancing bodies of those subjects whose political intervention has written upon the argument. On the other hand the argument unfolds on a stage – not necessarily a theatrical stage, but rather the space allowing for the meeting of two dancing subjects in embodied conversation. This chapter outlines the framework upon which the argument of the book is grounded.

Contraction and release

The first axis setting the boundaries for the choreographic outline of the argument is the tension between contraction and release. The tension between contraction and release has been problematised by Martha Graham, and her prism and interpretation will be discussed in Chapter 3 of this book. At this point, however, I outline this tension more broadly within my own choreographic-conceptual interpretation.

The argument examining political dance is placed within the motion between contraction and release and expounds on the physical significance of reflection on this conceptualisation. History is never experienced in a void; thinking about political dance entails listening to voices articulated through moving bodies that are asking us, as readers–spectators, to be heard. The argument is never metaphorical and always revisits a phenomenological moment. It is always thinking with and through bodies who have danced and who have registered their motion upon other bodies and upon this argument. At the same time the body of the argument dances, too, between contraction into the framework set forth by this book and release into the sources with which it converses; between affirming its own textual spatiality and relating itself to the interlocutors in the philosophical, choreographic, political and phenomenological locations it inhabits.

In the argument I explore the multi-dimensional self, entrenched in multiple symbolic webs expanding out to its embodied surroundings. This metaphor – which is never merely a metaphor – is entrenched in a normative assumption. Reading against the grain of textual analysis in political theory, I work to reposition dancing bodies that have written upon the pages of history but not always been carefully attended to. I contract into history in order to release the bodies that have been dancing on its margins. I hone the ears of the readers–spectators to listen more carefully to those voices that have been articulated and heard beyond words. Every dancing subject who speaks to me shows that for political conjunctions, human beings find manifold methods of self-expression. Further, subjects who are deemed marginal in politics in and through verbal language find creative and inspiring ways to show that they are never unequal to those who marginalise them. At times the most dire and seemingly hopeless situations give rise to novel and inventive ways of mobilising the human body. Thus contraction and release posit boundaries that are always expansive; boundaries that allow the body to transgress the space to which it had been assigned.

Contraction. The body watches within. It explores the registers of its own physicality. The body as a physical space is never one-dimensional; when contracting, the body expands into itself, unravelling new layers of meaning and new structures of signification. Contraction is a process of exploration within the body's spatiality; it is the marking of the dancer's physicality upon itself. Through contractions the dancing body reveals moments of equilibrium within the body that can be sustained. At the same time it also explores critical tensions within different levels of signification, which in turn push it towards another contraction. Contraction is a constant shift within, towards further moments of making sense to the embodied self through movement. In the contraction the dancer defines the boundaries of their choreographed world; but those boundaries within the body as a space shift with every new motion, with every further contraction, which goes deeper.

Identity is in flux, seeking moments of balance but always with the potential to shift towards new political gravitating forces. Those may be forces leading the body into moments of intervention, or rather, taking the body away towards quiet pause within.[1] This political-choreographic reading of contraction requires both motion and stillness; fall and recover; shifting and rest. Contractions allow the body to explore its own density; to investigate boundaries between inner and outer; and to investigate its relationality to other subjects, themselves undergoing the same motion. A danced contraction can never be repeated; there is a singular quality to the embodied investigation of the multifaceted body in a moment that cannot be repeated, as that body will not be the same in the next contraction. At the same time, the term 'contraction' affirms the rootedness of the body within its environment and its own embodied space. The body is first and foremost flesh, though it can appear weightless, fleshless. This process of the body making sense by unfolding into itself through acts of contraction necessarily relates to other bodies, as the body is part of a cobweb of signification. This shifts me into the second part of the first axis of the argument.

Release. Moments of release shift dancers from unravelling symbolic structures to themselves by shifting the single body towards other bodies in with which their bodies are in relationships. That relationality expands through instances of release. The spine unravels to the world around it; vertebra after vertebra, like a precious string of pearls, it opens up the body – as a space – to the space it inhabits. The body looks out, examining the inscriptions that are marked without, after shifting from within. When it is engaging those worlds the dancer inhabits, with a newfound physicality, marked by new systems of inscription, the dancer's body becomes a changed space by a multitude of contractions. The process of release constructs a world in the phenomenological space outside the body of the dancer. The body is always on stage, inhabiting worlds with others and moving towards them. Release is the process by which the dancer inhabits the phenomenological space around them and affirms that space as their world. However, the boundaries of this space are never stable; with every new moment of release the dancer shifts the boundaries of their bodies in space. They can expand the space their body takes in the world or reduce it; in either case the constitution of the world is a process of renegotiating boundaries in every movement.

Thus the first axis upon which the argument moves is the tension between contraction and release, an exploration of the politics of the moving body as an inscribed space and its relationality towards other bodies that it moves. The second axis, corresponding directly to the first axis and yet inhabiting a different register of my argument, is the political axis, which creates a distinction between two forms of danced politics: the weak reading of political dance and the strong reading of political dance. I move to explore this axis next.

The strong and weak readings of political dance

Throughout the book I trace moments in which dance interrupts words. To do so I cast the spotlight upon clashes between the strong reading of political dance and the weak reading of political dance.

I use the term 'weak reading of political dance' to refer to the use of dance to reiterate politics as articulated in words. This reading is termed 'weak' as it relies upon a different form of human expression to construct its logic; it cannot construct a world independently. Many of the studies which have inspired and galvanised this argument are grounded in this position. The edited collection *Dance and Politics* introduces itself as examining 'crises such as wars and revolutions as choreographic subject matter' (Kolb 2011: xiii) and explores diverse subject matter from Kurt Jooss's famous anti-war statement *The Green Table* (1932) through choreographic responses to anti-state terrorism (*Ulrike Meinhof* by Johann Kresnik), dance during the Second World War, and dance and rights (focusing on works such as Victoria Marks's *Not About Iraq* (2007)). All these analyses tackle choreographic works that have sought to elaborate and problematise issues discussed in words; very often, this is stated in the title of the piece. Kolb also states that the analyses in the book focus on twentieth- and early twenty-first-century Western stage dance (though she does leave some space for developments beyond it) (Kolb 2011: xiv). Randy Martin's *Performance as Political Act* is exemplary in its problematisation of the body in performance. His book *Critical Moves* has been groundbreaking in its approach to politics within dance studies. I discuss my conceptual relationship to his work under the next axis but here I note that his case studies are all from the context of American dance, from the Judson Church to his own participation in dance performances, *Last Supper in Uncle Tom's Cabin/The Promised Land* by Bill T. Jones (1990), multiculturalism and race within the United States, and a phenomenological study of a dance class. Again, whereas at times Martin (especially in the study of performance and rehearsal) allows for a reading of politics not iterated in words, the focus is even narrower than Kolb's book; it mostly looks at dance within New York City. Mark Franko's *Dancing Modernism/Performing Politics* as well as *Work of Labour* have been transformative for the approach I take, especially for my reading of the work of Martha Graham. At the same time, Franko focuses on dance for stage, too. As does André Lepecki, who rejuvenates the field substantially in his *Exhausting Dance*. All these texts will be discussed in the next axis of the argument. The edited collection *Dance, Human Rights, and Social Justice* diverges from the above sources in its wider international focus, and yet it limits its conceptual focus to issues around rights and right-claims rather than politics more broadly. Nevertheless, it has substantially inspired the last chapter of this book.

Set against the understanding of dance and politics that I term the weak reading of political dance is the strong reading of political dance, an interpretation of dance as a system of signification that sees its interlocutors as equal to speaking beings who use words; consequently dance is understood to be an independent system of signification that is enunciated and received without the need to be mediated by words. Bodies exploring their inner space unravel new possibilities for action through new symbolic configurations. Agents open up new worlds in motion, unravel crossroads between words and movement written on their bodies. Thus this distinction between the weak and strong reading of political dance is an epistemological one; the commitment towards the strong reading of political dance assumes that dance is a world that exists without requiring other forms of knowledge and being. For the subjects of this book, whose interventions in history have been written upon the argument, dance is a method of communicating; for those people who dance, moving in front of other bodies that are moved gives them a particular and unique mode of being, a singular moment of being alive, independent of other worlds they may inhabit. They require no other forms of communication to convey that unique mode of being.

At the same time, all human beings inhabit many worlds; thus the clash between these two readings of dance, of worlds independent of words and worlds in which words intersect with movement, allows us a unique glimpse into political dance. Hence throughout the book I examine moments of intersections between the weak and strong readings of political dance; moments in which dance acts independently of the words used to describe it. Dancers' bodies are also the pens with which they write upon other bodies. Reading dance as a language and a way of knowing means that the body is both the instrument of writing and the surface upon which it writes. Throughout the book I argue that the strong reading of political dance is intimately intertwined with the understanding of dance as an embodied language, a method of inscription independent of words. The third axis demarcating the argument is sic-sensuous, a concept which I utilise in order to focus upon acts of writing performed by manifold bodies who have written upon the argument; the argument in turn turns the spotlight on moments of shared sensation.

Sic-sensuous

The term 'sic' is used to refer to an apparent error of transcription; to indicate that a quote is recorded exactly as it is in the original. At the same time, dancers around the world are educated to fear the sickled foot, the unpointed foot turned in, perceived as the least beautiful use of the feet in classical ballet. The argument starts in the moment in which Isadora Duncan says 'no' to her ballet teacher; she refuses to stand on her toes. The refusal to abide by the rules of what is beautiful for Duncan is the catalyst for the unfolding of my argument. Throughout the book sic has a triple referent. First, I read sic as a refusal to abide by the rules of the beautiful or the aesthetically acceptable. Second, the term sic is always an act of writing: one body writing upon another body, and bodies writing upon their space. Third, the term sic refers to slippage of meaning, interventions and revolutions. The concept that may seem an error to one speaking being is another speaking being's method of expression. I am aided here by Anna Tsing's argument that global connection implies that 'words mean something different across a divide even when people agree to speak' (Tsing 2005: xi). Looking at connections between bodies across borders does not entail cohesive meaning; rather the focus is on those moments when signification is being negotiated in moments of slippage. The concept sic sheds conceptual light upon the body writing upon itself and other bodies in moments of aesthetic and political dissent between equal subjects. Thinking of dance through writing demands further investigation into deeper registers of the term sic and its use throughout the book, while releasing/turning towards other dance and political theorists who have considered the relationship between dance and writing.

Two books in particular have discussed inscription within the discipline of political theory and embodiment theory. Carrie Noland's *Agency and Embodiment: Performing Gestures/Producing Culture* discusses the communicative power of gesture and reinstates embodied discourses in a performative setting. She argues that gesture is a phenomenologically independent world constructed according to its own underlying principles (Noland 2009). Noland utilises the concept of inscription to understand gesture as a world: 'gestures are types of inscription, parsing of the body into signifying or operational units: they can thereby be seen to reveal the submission of a shared human anatomy to a set of bodily practices specific to one culture' (Noland 2009: 2). This account of inscription opens up the possibility of the body as an agency, actively writing upon another body and leaving its marks, which are always intertwined in its cultural symbolic web of signification. Noland concludes her book: 'I am suggesting that the gestural routines of inscription yield a kinaesthetic experience that is a resource in its own right, a resource of sensation capable of subverting the institutions of inscription by promising new, unmarked material to the world. ... the introspection provided by movement can be productive of new cultural meanings' (Noland 2009: 215). According to this reading, inscription allows for the creation of a symbolic world shared between bodies sharing sensation in movement when they create methods of being together. When thinking of inscription as a method of creating a shared sensation that does not correspond to institutionalised systems of power, we are presented with a new way of interpreting embodied practices – as providing alternative ways of being together through creating shared sensations. Noland's focus is on the independence of gesture and embodiment as a self-disclosing world. In that world created by inscription people interact with each other without requiring other systems of communication. It may be true that bodies interact without words; but it is also widely accepted that human communication is mainly effected through words. The challenge of my own framework is to understand inscription as enabling the creation of a world of shared sensation but also to show that it has interrupted political discourse occurring in words.

Erin Manning in *Politics of Touch* uses tango as an example throughout her analysis. Indeed, the tango becomes much more than an example; it becomes a prism through which she inquires about the possibilities of a sensed body in movement (Manning 2007). She sees tango as opening up the way for engaging a cultural phenomenon which is both nationalistic and inventive. She finds that dance allows the creation of two worlds in parallel. At the same time, she writes, 'the body cannot be reduced to language' (Manning 2007: 58). Manning understands language here as necessarily reductive and in a tension between invention and political structure (in this quotation, nationalism).

Eminent dance theorist Randy Martin has provided a beautifully articulated definition of dance:

> dance is best understood as a kind of embodied practice that makes manifest how movement comes to be by momentarily concentrating and elaborating in one place forces drawn from beyond a performance setting. The constituent features of any given dance work include technical proclivities and aesthetic sensibilities that elaborate and depend on aspects of physical culture and prevailing ideologies. (Martin 1998: 5)

This conceptualisation shifts between moments of concertation of energy and its release. The body is inscribed within the space it inhabits and at the same time the body as a space corresponds to the space it inhabits. Moreover, dance has a continuous element within it even when it is rapturous and disturbing. Dance as a world inscribes upon the bodies of its participants – audience members and spectators alike – and changes their embodied spatiality after they leave the theatre.

Martin argues that taking dance seriously aids us in going beyond the despair of an arrested present towards thinking about an enriched social life. Further, 'if one grants that along with dance, politics cannot have a solitary form or a unitary object, if neither can be one thing or about one thing, it becomes possible to notice a proliferation of political activity throughout the social fabric and not simply confined to what are formally considered to be political institutions' (Martin 1998: 2). Inspired by Martin, I argue that dance is a source of possibility in opening new futures and creating new disagreements within our existing political present. Dance enables its participants to unravel a new world, offering new opportunities for its participants. Those opportunities may be inhibited in other political worlds they occupy.

Martin reads technique as a site in which mastery of the body in other sites in society becomes manifest. This is a very severe and dark reading of technique. At the same time he acknowledges that technique is an essential part of dance. He writes: 'at the most general level, technique brings together the practical accomplishment of a given activity with the means to regulate what is considered appropriate to that activity' (Martin 1998: 20). Technique, in this reading, is a space in which the body is mastered and disciplined. Technique cannot be utilised towards possibilities of further subversion. It belongs to an arrested present, not to an unfolding future. There is no space for error and intervention; for slippage of meaning and reinterpretation by the recipient body. The discourse only works on the body inwards; the body does not write back on its own spatiality or on other bodies. However, other scholars who engage in technique move us from this severe reading of technique towards a less grim interpretation of its use in allowing repetition of performance to occur.

One such scholar, Jill Green, writes: 'while dance educators may be attempting to "free" students through an arts education based on the techniques of modern dance pioneers such as Martha Graham and Merce Cunningham, whose techniques offer an expressive means to communicate art, they may not be aware of how power actually plays out in the dance classroom' (Green 2002–3: 120). Green places Graham and Cunningham outside of her otherwise grim reading of technique as repressive. She reads their technique as a way to bring the inner subjectivity towards a communal, shared space. This critique enables us to challenge the dichotomies of technique/expression and power/communication. Green's reading of Martha Graham's contribution to the world of dance simultaneously includes all of the above and is different from reading dance technique as purely disciplinary. Dance technique can be perceived, in her own words, as an expressive means to communicate art. At the same time this reading unravels another way to think about dance and inscription more broadly, utilising this interpretation without privileging Graham and Cunningham. I interpret dance as entrenched in technique, which allows it to occur beyond a single performance in a more egalitarian way and utilise the analytic structure beyond Graham's privileged bodies.

Mark Franko's work on the politics of the choreography of Isadora Duncan and Martha Graham is of great importance to my reading of these choreographers' work. In his analysis of neo-classical choreographer William Forsythe, Franko discusses the 'reflexivity built into dance that is more complex than the phenomenon of inscription that usually dominates discussions of power and agency with respect to the body in his work' (Franko 2011: 105). He suggests another way to understand embodiment in dance, drawing on Foucault, when he reads embodiment as 'the performance of a discursive practice with and through the body rather than as the effect of that discourse's inscription on the same body or on two bodies as equals' (Franko 2011: 103). Franko's reading of discourse enables a re-evaluation of the concept of inscription, one that accounts for a body's ability to write on other bodies, thereby creating an inscribed dialogue through the equality of those two bodies. The use of both 'with and through' here suggests a multitude of ways to engage one's body within the practice of dance. I push this reading further by turning to Susan Leigh Foster's argument regarding the body as writing and written upon. She argues that this reading of complexity within embodiment enables agency or resistance in forms of cultural production (Foster 1995). The idea of dance as a discursive practice opens the possibility of another reading of inscription, as one body acting upon another equal body, rather than a reading of the body as a docile materiality written upon by networks by which it has been disciplined. This reading of egalitarian inscription allows for a reading of a dancing body creating a world sustained beyond one singular performance and intervening in configurations of power rather than being controlled by them. The body as a space can intervene in the phenomenological space it occupies and not just inhabit it.

André Lepecki, whose book *Exhausting Dance: Performance and the Politics of Movement* develops a unique approach, writes, 'body and

language fuse one into the other to display modes of subjectivization'
(Lepecki 2006: 55). Language and embodiment are no longer orthogo-
nal to each other, and the dialogue between them produces a concept of
embodied language. Lepecki invokes here Foucault's famous 'the body is
the inscribed surface of events' (Lepecki 2006: 55). Thus Lepecki brings
the conception of dance as an embodied language together with the concept of inscription. This approach is elaborated further in a close reading of contemporary French choreographer Jerome Bel: 'the body, in its
most visceral activation, is not only a surface of inscription, as Foucault
noted, but an instrument of writing, an inassimilable agent that constantly writes history back' (Lepecki 2006: 57). Inscription is understood
as a multi-dimensional body responding to another multi-dimensional
body grounded in these bodies' equality. Most profoundly, this lesson is
learned from the work of a choreographer rather than any textual interpretation. It is Bel's work that teaches Lepecki the power of inscription;
it is Bel's body inscribing upon Lepecki that in turn inscribes upon his
book. The body is a pen that can write on another body serving as paper.
But they are always first and foremost equal spaces.

When Lepecki discusses technique he writes:

> for it's precisely dance's self-depiction as a lamentably ephemeral art form,
> the melancholic drive at its core, that generates systems and performances
> of high reproducibility: strict techniques named after dead masters applied
> to carefully selected bodies, continuous modelling of bodies through endless
> repetition of exercises, dieting, surgeries, the perpetuation of systems of racial
> exclusion for the sake of 'proper' visibility, an endemic eruption of archival
> fevers, the international and transcultural spreading of national ballets per-
> forming nineteenth century steps for the sake of dancing their status as mod-
> ern nations. (Lepecki 2006: 126)

Here we see Lepecki departing from his three-dimensional notion of
inscription and revisiting the idea of dead masters controlling docile
bodies. At the same time, shifting an ethical position yields a different
conceptual interpretation of inscription. If we consider technique in a
more egalitarian way, as Lepecki suggested earlier, and regard inscription
as one body writing on another in the act of dance, understanding all
bodies as equal tools for writing, we gain new insights into the interpretation of inscription discussed throughout the book.

Dance intervenes in other systems of signification and affirms the
equality of its interlocutors. Thus it creates a sic-sensuous between communication through the body and communication in words; a world in
which the former is received as equal to verbal language and a world in

which it is not. I see all dancing bodies as equal; Martha Graham equal to the dancer in a flash mob. This interpretation is intimately related to the tension between contraction and release. The body is part of a cobweb of signification. Dancers shift from unravelling symbolic structures to themselves, to revealing those networks of signification to other bodies in which they occupy relational spaces, never alone. That relationality expands through instances of release. The process of release constructs a world in the phenomenological space outside the body of the dancer. It is the process by which the dancer inhabits the phenomenological space around them and affirms that space as their world. However, the boundaries of this space are never stable; with every new moment of release the dancer shifts the boundaries of their bodies in space towards the physical world and their fellow dancers and spectators. They can expand the space their body takes in the world or reduce it; in either case the constitution of the world is a process of renegotiating boundaries in every movement. This leads me from the concept of sic, writing on the body by the body, to the concept of sensuous.

The body in my reading of dance is both sensual and sensed; it creates meaning for itself as well as for others. My reading of Carrie Noland's *Agency and Embodiment* gives the theoretical framework an important register. Noland analyses gesture, which she sees as affording an opportunity for kinaesthetic introspective experience as well as influencing cultural practice (Noland 2009). She discusses gestures as creating kinaesthetic experiences while being performed. For Noland, gestures enable a moment of kinaesthetic embodied reflection in movement. At the same time, revisiting Manning's work on tango yields a relational aspect to this part of the argument: focusing on touch, Manning argues that it is both the creation of a world but also always relational: 'I reach out to touch you in order to invent a relation that will, in turn, invent me' (Noland 2009: xv). This interpretation considers an embodied experience which is self-reflexive and simultaneously relational, influencing other bodies with which the body interacts. The relationship between reflexivity and relationality as an essential part of the body in movement shifts the argument towards the concept of kinaesthetic empathy, which has been central in dance studies throughout the twentieth century.

Influential dance critic John Martin, whose comments on the work of Martha Graham will be discussed in Chapter 3 of this book, writes:

> when we see a human body moving, we see movement which is potentially produced by any human body, and therefore by our own ... through kinaesthetic sympathy we actually reproduce it vicariously in our present muscular

experience and awaken such associational connotations as might have been ours if the original movement had been of our own making. (Foster 2011: 117)

This conception of two bodies mirroring each other's movement has stirred much discussion in dance studies. Dee Reynolds and Matthew Reason understand kinaesthetic empathy in its strongest form to include imagining the substitution of one agent for another; 'for a fleeting moment, perhaps, I simulate your action, and in so doing I imagine I occupy your place' (Reynolds and Reason 2012: 125). Embodied empathy is understood here as a moment in which the boundary between two bodies becomes transcendent: one subject is able to physically imagine itself as another. One body is able to displace the boundaries of its own sensed body. They note that 'the dance spectator can be invested as both subject and object in a shared materiality and flow of choreographed movement across dancers' bodies ... and that certain techniques and choreographic approaches are particularly conducive to this experience' (Reynolds and Reason 2012: 129). The emphasis here is on sharing and the transitivity of sensation from one moving body to another rather than mirroring motion as discussed by Martin. Further, Reynolds notes that there are some choreographic techniques that are able to induce this experience more than others.

Susan Leigh Foster criticises John Martin's interpretation of kinaesthetic empathy, especially from a political-normative perspective that exposes its biases. Martin saw African-American artist Peal Primus as 'true to herself both individually and as an individual artist' (Foster 2011: 161). At the same time, Martha Graham was perceived by him to be able to absorb rhythms of Native Americans. Leigh Foster argues that the white, and for Martin racially unmarked, body of Graham could feel free to absorb and draw from the rhythms specific to racially marked people, whereas the black body struggled under dual responsibilities to art and race. Leigh Foster goes on to conclude that Martin's theory reiterated the exclusions and double standards that placed the white body as unmarked, and repositioned the white, middle-class body as the universal body that could feel into and for all of the other bodies with which it was in relationships. Leigh Foster then offers her own interpretation of the concept of kinaesthetic empathy. She argues that empathetic connections demonstrate the many ways in which the kinaesthetic body in its particularity appeals to viewers who apprehend the dance. Consequently this interpretation of kinaesthetic empathy illuminates what is at the heart of shared embodied experience. At the same time she writes that 'by inviting viewers into a specific experience of what the body is, they also enable us to contemplate how the body is grounded, its function in remembering, its affinity with cultural values, its participation in the construction of gender and sexuality, and the ways in which it is assimilating technologies so as to change the very definition of the human' (Foster 2011: 218). Leigh Foster's reading exposes both the particularity of the bodies which are creating a discursive act and the shared essence that allows that discursive act to take place. This reading, then, through its conception of kinaesthetic empathy, brings into conceptual focus both difference and similarity, and allows for a more egalitarian conception of kinaesthetic empathy, as distinct from one universal, privileged body which creates the conditions for sharing. This reading also notes the various categories that deem some bodies to be unequal and the way these inequalities may be reproduced under the guise of universality. It asks us to be attentive to the body's situatedness within the cultural-symbolic framework and at the same time draws upon a shared conception of embodiment that allows those differences to appear.

In her seminal work *The Human Condition* Hannah Arendt writes:

> If men were not equal, they could neither understand each other and those who came before them nor plan for the future and foresee the needs of those who will come after them. If men were not distinct, each human being distinguished from any other who is, or ever will be, they would need neither speech nor action to make themselves understood. (Arendt 1998: 176)

I draw on Arendt's formulation to move my own reading of shared embodied space a step further within the concept of sic-sensuous. Using Arendt's formulation regarding language, I read dance as an embodied language. I see moments of empathy in dance performance enabling the transgression of boundaries between the self and other; I see these moments of shared sensation as enabling the experience of both that which is shared communally and that which constructs each body in its unique symbolic space. Thus those moments of shared sensation through the sensuous body illuminate the dissimilarities between human bodies sharing those spaces; but this process is enabled because of the underlying equality between all bodies. In this conception the shared sensuous is a space in which bodies experience a contradiction between their equality and their difference; between their presentation as equal and conditions of life outside of theatre that render them as unequal. This conception of shared sensation, in turn, allows us also to understand better those conditions that render the white, middle-class, heteronormative body as universal; at the same time it seeks moments in which other bodies have responded to that claim and showed their difference.

In that moment, I argue that they have showed that they are equal after all. Thus the emphasis is always on the sensuous body that is able to share sensation with another sensuous body. At the same time this moment of sharing, just like the linguistic conjuncture problematised by Arendt, illuminates the uniqueness and particularity of both those bodies, each engraved by different symbolic inscriptions, inscribed by different worlds that sometimes do not intersect in verbal language. This moves me to contract further, into the conceptual framework with which I work throughout the book.

Conceptual framework

1. The plurality and difference between human beings manifests itself in the fact that different people find different methods for self-expression. Not all political issues are manifested or articulated through verbal language: seeking objects of study outside of verbal language enhances our understanding of what can be termed political and thus gives a clearer picture of the pluralism underlying human life. There are more languages than just verbal language; human beings have found manifold ways to communicate with each other.
2. Dance is an embodied language, a form of communication between bodies in motion. As such, it adheres to different rules and structures than those of verbal language. Understanding dance as a method of communication brings into the political conversations between those subjects who, through an embodied method of self-expression, were not listened to when politics is understood solely through verbal language. Dance is the way those subjects perform their equality to those expressing themselves through verbal language.
3. There are some instances in which some human beings are marginalised by depriving them of access to spoken language. Some people have been – and indeed still are – deemed unequal by placing them outside of a verbally constructed public sphere.
4. There are clashes between verbal and non-verbal languages. In the meeting point between dance and verbal languages we see the collision between the different symbolic and political frameworks underscoring those two forms of languages. At the same time those clashes outline the different positions subjects may occupy in those different worlds; they may be deemed equal in one world and marginal in another.

5. Hence, the conceptual focus in the book is on clashes between what I term the weak reading of political dance – the use of dance to rearticulate the meaning of ideas discussed in verbal language – and the strong reading of political dance – dance expressing the meaning of political ideas independently of verbal language.

6. The strong reading of political dance, or the constitution of dance as a world that does not require language, provides a moment of shared embodied space between the dancer and the spectator. That is a moment in which two bodies, one on stage and one in the audience, share an embodied space. This moment does not mean the dancer and spectator share the same sensation but rather the shared sensation illuminates the fact that the body of the dancer is equal to that of the spectator; hence it is able to generate sensation in that moved body.

7. That shared moment is a meeting point between equality and plurality; it is the equality of bodies that allows them to speak with each other, unmediated by words; and at the same time it is the plurality of human beings that pushes them to express themselves through their bodies. The argument steers away from the affirmation of sameness or universality in those moments of shared sensation. Thus the strong reading of political dance allows for the possibility of the performance of a clash between equality and difference.

8. Dance as a world allows itself to be repeated beyond a singular performance through inscription. In the moment of performance the embodied act inscribes upon the body of the speaker as well as upon the body of the recipient. This conception of inscription is understood through an egalitarian prism. Inscription in dance is utilised by celebrated choreographers and untrained dancers alike. This interpretation of inscription includes both the intentional messages conveyed by dancers and choreographers and slippages of meaning occurring through misinterpretations and aesthetic ruptures.

9. Dance inscribes upon the body. Because the body can be altered by new methods of inscription it allows the subject to know about their communities and possibilities. In its ability to open up new worlds of meaning the body can open up new possibilities of being in the world, new spaces in which the subject can partake.

10. A dancing body is never alone; it is always conversing with an Other. The tension between contraction and release is the tension between the world of the dancer within her own body and her relationships with other dancing bodies.

11. The first axis upon which the argument is constructed is the tension between contraction and release.
12. The second axis upon which the argument is constructed is the tension between the strong reading of political dance – moments in which dance communicates through bodies messages that were not articulated in words uttered about that dance – and their clashes with dance reinterpreted in words.
13. The third axis upon which the argument is constructed is the axis of sic-sensuous – the process of inscription by which one sensed body writes upon another. That movement that is considered not-beautiful may be the method by which its creators unfold a world in which they perform their equality to those who see them as marginal. The sickled foot may be the way a dancer performs their subjectivity and articulates their equality to those dead masters who have told her 'it is not beautiful'.
14. In its constant motion between contraction and release, in moments of sic-sensuous and clashes between the strong and weak readings, dance enables performers and spectators to transcend their embodied boundaries qua subjects. Thus the definition of a dancing subject is never a stable one. The body is a space in and of itself that in the process of inscribing upon itself in dance realises its openendedness. The subject never arrives at a stable destination; it keeps contesting its own embodied boundaries. This shifting position stands in sharp contrast to the fact that the subject may be forcefully grounded in small demarcated spaces in other symbolic systems. Thus there is possibility for interruption and rupture in a world that is always in becoming. This becomes particularly significant when subjects inhabiting that world are constituted as stable – and marginal – within other worlds they inhabit.
15. Dancing subjects can transcend the boundaries of their communities.
15a. Dancing subjects can live in more than one world – they can be subjects in both the world constituted by dance as a method of communication and the world constituted by words as a method of expression.
15b. As their bodies are never stable and their bodies are spaces that can become changed by various methods of inscription, dancing bodies can occupy a space larger than the one assigned to them in politics which is carried out in words.
16. As a practice that goes beyond boundaries, dance can challenge boundaries that demarcate communities through verbal language. The space created by dance may transcend spaces created by words.

Within the moment in which dancers belong to a community larger than the one they were assigned to and prove that they are equal despite not being interpreted as such, dance has the potential to transcend boundaries of communities demarcated in and through verbal language.

17. Constructing the argument between these three axes (weak–strong political dance; sic-sensuous relationality of bodies; and contraction – challenging the boundaries of bodies inwards – and release – challenging the boundaries of bodies outward) gives it a three-dimensional space. The argument is never without a space; it unfolds first and foremost in the dancing body; then on the stage, either literally or metaphorically, upon which that dancing body performs in front of another body. The first body from which the argument unfolds is that of modern dance pioneer, Isadora Duncan. I allow her to take her position centre stage first.

Note

1   Here I am inspired by T. S. Eliot's *Four Quartets*, which will be revisited in my analysis of Martha Graham:

> At the still point of the turning world. Neither flesh nor fleshless;
> Neither from nor towards; at the still point, there the dance is,

2

'I dreamed of a different dance':
Isadora Duncan's danced revolution

Modern dance innovator Isadora Duncan (1877–1927) truly moved beyond boundaries, both choreographically and politically. Born in San Francisco, then dancing with Augustine Daly Dance Theatre in 1896, she moved from London to Paris to Berlin in quick succession, performing in salons and achieving success before the age of twenty. In 1905 she established her first school in Germany, aimed at children of all classes, and in 1914 she went to the US and transferred her school there. Duncan founded a school for working-class children in Germany in 1915, and after the revolution in Russia she unsurprisingly moved there in 1921, where she felt she could bring her political and aesthetic vision to fruition. Her understanding of class politics was inseparable from her interpretation of other forms of oppression, and those different categories become intermingled in her interpretation of dance. She was a radical on more than one plane.[1]

She returned to the West in 1925, and after a tour of Germany she settled in Paris. She died in Nice on 14 September 1927, when her shawl got tangled in the wheel of a car and she broke her spine.

Duncan's work was always entrenched in the social conditions of her time. Her reception, I will show, was intertwined with the tensions of a woman whose existence brought the dance of the future to the present, when the present wasn't always ready to fully comprehend her. Duncan lived her life between worlds; at the same time the main tool for intervention was her own body, thus she was never without a world. Isadora Duncan's performance arc is an instance par excellence of sic-sensuous and a clash between the weak and strong readings of political dance.

Ann Daly, who has written extensively on Duncan, divides her choreographic life into several periods. The first period (1908–11) centred around the image of Duncan as the young nymph, an image that endured in her historiography. In this period she explored the fluidity of movement and based her dancing on physical release. The second period (1914–18) is characterised by her exploration of heroic and at times nationalistic themes, from Greek myth (*Iphigenia*, 1915) to her famous rendition of *Marseillaise* (1914). The third period, occurring around her time in the Soviet Union (1922–3), saw a monumental Isadora who was barely moving, exploring the movement of her stillness (Daly 1995).

Duncan's intervention, as well as its reception, is entangled in resisting the bounded spaces which were allocated for her. She was never afraid of saying no to aesthetic and social constraints. Her choreographic development is inseparable from her involvement in bringing her body to centre stage, creating a space in which it was perceived as legitimate and she is interpreted as a legible subject. Consequently she unravelled numerous spheres of resistance to those who followed her. Duncan's interpretation of her own embodiment in bringing her body to performance anticipates what will later be interpreted as radical feminism, understanding women's oppression and marginalisation as occurring in further and more clandestine ways than mere legal structures.[2] Let Isadora Duncan enter centre stage of the argument; I invite the reader–spectator to take their seat in a performance taking place on 7 October 1922.

'I am a revolutionary: all great artists are revolutionaries': Isadora Duncan's strong reading of political dance

Isadora Duncan performs in her homeland of America. She returns to the US after having spent a year in Soviet Russia. Before the tour starts she is detained with her husband, Serge Esenin, on Ellis Island. She is already famous across the globe and her relationship with Russia makes her both intriguing and threatening to American audiences.

The programme is danced to Tchaikovsky with his 6th Symphony (the *Pathétique*) and *Marche Slave*. Those are two of her more 'monumental' works, different from the evanescent Schubert and Chopin pieces which brought her fame in early phases of her career. In Boston, the performance ends in an explosive and rapturous way, retold in multiple narratives. The most recurrent one is that she waves her red silk scarf over her head and says: 'This is red! So am I! It is the colour of life and vigour. You were once wild here. Don't let them tame you!' From thereon we encounter a contradictory and problematic moment of reception. I pause here with some accounts of this performance which do not fully agree. Peter Kurth's biography presents a piece from the *Chicago Tribune* on 23 October:

in concluding one of the most amazing performances ever witnessed in Boston, Isadora Duncan, modern originator of the classical dance, waved a flaming red scarf which a moment before had been part of her costume ... and shouted 'This is red! That is what I am!' She shook the symbol of revolt in the faces of the spectators, most of whom were standing, and cried, 'don't let them tame you!' (Kurth 2002: 519)

Kurth also notes the disagreement over what happened in that exact performance: some claim she waved a red scarf over her head; some critics claim one of her breasts was revealed, either in dance or when she extended her hand to end the performance; some accounts, however, claimed she tore her tunic and revealed her breasts to the audience. Ilya Ilitch Schneider, who helped Duncan on behalf of the People's Commissar for Education to adjust to Moscow when she first arrived, notes this incident with no reference to nudity, merely to 'waving the scarf and shouting "I am red"' (Schneider 1968: 122). Irma Duncan quotes Isadora as saying 'this is red! So am I! it is the colour of life and vigour. You were once wild here. Don't let them tame you' (referencing only waving the scarf) (Duncan 1929: 164). Irma Duncan notes the offence caused by this statement and the fact that some people left the performance. Irma Duncan quotes the headline 'Red dancer shocks Boston. Isadora's speech drives many from Boston hall. Duncan, in flaming red scarf, says she's red' (Duncan 1929: 165). She notes the slippage in some accounts into tearing her whole dress off and delivering the entire speech in the nude. Colin Chambers, who has written extensively upon Duncan's politics, argues that she tore her tunic while denying deliberately mismanaging her garments (Chambers 2006).

Regardless of what exactly happened on 7 October 1922, there were two direct consequences of that performance. Isadora Duncan was banned from performing in Boston by the mayor, James M. Curely, under Boston's decency laws. At the same time Kurth notes that she responded to the discussion around this performance with the statement: 'if my Art is symbolic of any one thing it is symbolic of the freedom of woman and her emancipation from the hidebound conventions that are the warp and weft of New England puritanism' (Kurth 2002: 521). Through her offensiveness – on the grounds either of communist references or of exposing her body – Isadora Duncan was able to claim her space as a legitimate speaking subject by showing the intertwining of her political and choreographic goals. She carved this space in the action of waving that red scarf, far more significant than the lethal scarf that will be entangled in the memory of her death.

This performance in 1922 exemplifies what I read as sic-sensuous. Duncan performs her radicalism here; she is so radical that the mayor of Boston himself intervenes in her plans for performance. Moreover, the entanglement of seeing the performance as 'vulgar' and offensive because of her socialist convictions shows the entanglement of the aesthetic and the political. What is perceived as 'ugly' is seen so in proximity to, if not entanglement with, political offence. And all this was brought about by a clash of two sensuous bodies, the body of the spectator and the body of Isadora Duncan.

In a statement from 1922 Duncan says: 'I am not a politician. I am an artist. But I will try in my dancing to help America to understand the magnificent spirit of Russia' (Duncan 1994: 69). This statement, as well as the political controversy presented above, gains further meaning when read in the context of one of Duncan's essays, the 'Philosopher's Stone of Dancing':

> There are ... three kinds of dancers: first, those who consider dancing as a sort of gymnastic drill, made up of impersonal and graceful arabesques; second, those who, by concentrating their minds, lead the body into the rhythm of a desired emotion, expressing a remembered feeling or experience. And finally, there are those who convert the body into a luminous fluidity, surrendering it to the inspiration of the soul. This third sort of dancer understands that the body, by force of the soul, can in fact be converted to a luminous fluid. The flesh becomes light and transparent, as shown through the X-ray, but with the difference that the human soul is lighter than these rays. (Duncan 1977: 51)

Ann Daly interprets the 'third dancer' as someone who expresses 'all humanity, something greater than all selves' (Daly 1995: 136). Duncan refuses to endorse a dancer who is committed to a remembered feeling, to an already known system of symbols. She prefers the sort of dance that gives motion to something radically new, going beyond known meanings and emotions. Chambers writes further: 'she believed in the culture of the body ... Politics for her was not a means to an end but an inspiration for the performer to question ceaselessly' (Chambers 2006: 93). I understand Duncan's choreographic intervention as a sic-sensuous between the three dancers. Her choreographic intervention enabled her to present the third dancer as opposed to the first dancer (who, as we will see, is based upon her reading of ballet). At the same time, the third dancer allows Duncan to dissent from the second dancer, who represents known feelings and ideas; in a political context that means reiterating ideologies and thoughts as articulated in words or what we have described as the weak political reading of dance. In fact, she herself defended this reading of her work as enabling two worlds to collide when she was challenged about her musical choices: 'When she was going to dance the "Marche Slave" (1917), she was told she could not because it contained extracts from the Tsarist national anthem. She won the argument that the (musical) piece itself was not important but her treatment was' (Chambers 2006: 77). Dance for Duncan has a power independent of other means of communication and indeed can transgress those symbolic systems. She is committed to legitimising the strong political reading of dance.

After contracting into Duncan's body as the 'third dancer' we release into the experience of being her spectator at that performance in 1922, sharing an embodied space with Isadora Duncan. Duncan's reception as offensive – either as 'red' or as naked – shows where her political transgression lies. She presents her body as equal where it has no space yet to be received as such; moreover, in that act of dissent, she claims that space for other bodies to be received as equal. Duncan was offensive because in her embodied performance she dared to be equal; equal as a female body taking public space, and equal as a woman re-signifying perceptions of society in her treatment of all women and men as appropriate recipients of her choreographic revolution. Isadora Duncan's relationship to equality cannot be understood by singular categories such as feminism or socialism; she demanded equality in every moment in which she performed and exhibited her radically new language of movement. Indeed, we must understand her revolution in categories that she constituted through dance. Let us once again contract into Isadora Duncan's body in her moment of aesthetic revolution, which changed the world of modern dance as it is known to us today.

The woman who danced the chorus: intervention and inscription

I turn to two paragraphs from Isadora Duncan's autobiography in order to examine her aesthetic break in her own language:

> When the teacher told me to stand on my toes, I asked him why, and he replied, 'because it is beautiful', and I said it was ugly and against nature and after the third class left never to return. The stiff and commonplace gymnastics which he called dancing only disturbed my dream. I dreamed of a different dance. I did not know just yet what it would be, but I was feeling out towards an invisible world into which I divined I might enter if I found the key. (Duncan 1995: 22)

Further:

> I spent long days and nights in the studio seeking that dance that can be the divine expression of the human spirit through the medium of the body's movement. For hours I would stand quite still, my two hands folded between my breasts, covering the solar plexus … I was seeking, and finally discovered, the central spring of all movement, the creator of motor power, the unity from which all diversions of movements are born, the mirror of vision for the creation of dance – it was from this discovery that was born the theory upon which I have founded my school. (Duncan 1995: 58)

Isadora Duncan, the dance student, is told to imitate the prevalent aesthetic. Her teacher brings her into an embodied conversation with the 'first dancer'. Her body is becoming inscribed with the symbolic framework which defined what dance is taken to mean in her contemporary world – that aesthetic which she sees as 'commonplace gymnastics'. But she refuses to become fully inscribed with this language. She rejects the ethos of the beautiful as the rationale determining what dance is and, moreover, what it could be. Thus this is a double interruptive gesture: she interrupts the ballet class because traditional conceptualisation of dance galvanises her to find the third dancer, discussed above. She also interrupts the structure of authority in which she is supposed to abide by the logic and structure of dance provided for her by her teacher. The woman student says no to the male dance teacher. No categories which place Isadora Duncan's body in a demarcated space can be sustained for her. The third dancer provides Duncan with a new way to dance, arising from the body and speaking to the body, and unbound by previous aesthetics which are always rooted in the social and political conditions of her time. When Isadora Duncan says no to her ballet teacher, she refuses many structures of authority underpinning that relationship. She creates a moment of sic-sensuous in motion.

Further, Duncan's method of unravelling the dancer of the future within herself is to allow her body to experiment with various techniques of inscribing upon itself. Her process of emancipation of herself from the world of ballet in which her teacher is so deeply entrenched, as well as from the social and political world in which she experiences multiple inequalities,[3] is to open up a world which draws upon her own body and elaborates her own independent aesthetic. This reaction was based on the discovery of the solar plexus as the centre of the body, a technical reinterpretation which was of prime significance for Duncan as well as for her students and audiences. The method by which Duncan extends her aesthetic break to others is to contract into her own body as a world, inhabiting the space she occupies; the sharing with others begins by releasing the movement to those around her.

Duncan dancer Julia Levien writes about the process of preparation in the Duncan technique: 'place right hand over the solar plexus area' (Levien 1994: 2); 'it must be emphasised that every movement emerges both physically and emotively from the body centre – "the solar plexus" – and that radiates outward to become part of the surrounding space, both immediate and limitless' (Levien 1994: xii). She writes:

> 'all movements must come from the centre', Isadora taught. That centre is located physically in what we call 'the solar plexus'. Anatomically, it is the muscle belt of the diaphragm, which controls the breath and reacts, both by expanding positively and contracting negatively, according to the variety of emotions imposed on it. (Levien 1994: 1)

A Duncan technique class starts from what Irma Duncan calls 'a natural position' (Duncan 1970: 1). She continues that an opening position starts with a 'solar plexus drawn ... anatomically, all our muscles run obliquely towards a centre-point, the solar plexus' (Duncan 1970: 2, 11). Chambers also argues that Isadora Duncan created with her body from the solar plexus (Chambers 2006). This use of the solar plexus is understood as Duncan's clearest rejection of ballet technique. Her moment of dissent against ballet as a technique, crystallised by her embodied reinterpretation of the solar plexus, is communicated further: her students share her moment of dissent with her and communicate it to other students, and thus the embodied conversation continues. The Duncan dance student shares the process of investigating the solar plexus; the bodies of Duncan students are inscribed in Isadora Duncan's moment of dissent. The third dancer, Duncan's own body responding to ballet as a system of signification, discovers her solar plexus as the spring of the new symbolic system which is communicated to others. To return to Isadora Duncan's own writing: 'when I have danced I have tried always to be the Chorus: I have been the Chorus of young girls hailing the return of the fleet, I have been the Chorus dancing the Pyrrhic Dance, or the Bacchic; I have never once danced a solo' (Duncan 1977: 96). The third dancer is never alone. She contracts into her own body but at the same time releases into others. The boundaries of her body are porous to other bodies upon which she will inscribe; thus she creates a system of inscription that is also a shared embodied space. Isadora Duncan allows her moment of dissent – against politics articulated in words as well as against ballet as the prevailing aesthetic of her time – to transcend the boundaries of her own body when she creates an ever-expanding chorus of movement. Duncan's intervention into the world of body is inscribed upon her body and is a response to other systems of signification inscribed upon her body; in the moment of interruption she creates her own method of inscription, released into a shared space inhabited by other bodies.

This moment of dance as sharing an inscribed embodied space transcends Duncan and her dancers. It is also of paramount importance for Isadora Duncan's conception of spectatorship. Mark Franko discusses the fact that through the solar plexus Duncan strived to create a connection between herself as dancer and the audience: 'it put her audience in direct and unmediated contact with meaning "in person"' (Franko 1995: 2). Ann Daly argues that the kinaesthetic appeal of Duncan dance involved the response of the whole body, not just the eye, and by so doing enabled the spectators to feel that they are participating in the performance, by 'moving' with Duncan (Daly 1992). Duncan opened up a moment of embodied sharing between herself and her audience; that moment of embodied sharing utilised the concept of the solar plexus, which has also been central in the moment in which she intervenes against ballet. Her moment of sic-sensuous is never without a space and is written upon her own body as well as other bodies into which she releases, whether those of her students or audience members. Duncan's dance was aimed at creating shared embodiment, and this was enabled through the exploration of the solar plexus. Isadora Duncan's dissenting body, discovering the solar plexus, inscribes this moment of intervention upon her students' bodies; those bodies in turn inscribe this moment of dissent through galvanising the solar plexus to create a focal point in the shared embodied space they unravel. When Isadora Duncan claimed she never danced a solo it is because her body was always aimed at an Other – student or spectator; it was galvanised to share her embodied space. Let us now contract once again into Duncan's space of intervention: her dancing body.

Musical Moment (circa 1907)

Music: Franz Schubert, Moment Musicale, D. 780, Op. 94, No. 3 (www.youtube.com/watch?v=Kq2GgIMMo60)

One of Duncan's earliest works, this is a playful piece of movement which exemplifies her method of inscription. The dance as it is viewed here – faithful to the original version – is performed as a solo piece which constantly moves in space, shifting back and forth in a movement that creates a slight circle on stage. The spatial configuration of the dance is circular and flowing, reflecting its choreographic language. The dancer's body releases into space-time only to contract back to where she had started.

Much attention is paid to hand gestures and their use to create the illusion of pause, whilst the movement itself never really ceases, adding to the feeling of circularity. The tension between the hops and hand gestures in the dance encapsulates the tension between repetition (repeating of hops) and interruption (in hand gestures). With the hand gestures and the movement in space the dancer never really stops. The flowing musicality of the piece guides its choreographic narrative, as the dancer echoes the shift between a resolution of a musical phrase and its consequent contestation. The music determines the language and logic of the piece.

The dance moves between hesitation and affirmation, lightness and decision. The dancer seems light, almost bodiless; she shifts in space with purpose disguised by ephemeral movement. The movement shifts towards the audience and back into upstage, the part of the stage furthest from the audience. Duncan dancer Sylvia Gold, who worked with both Elisabeth Duncan and Irma Duncan, writes about Musical Moment: 'This dance is probably the most difficult dance to perform well. The feeling of surprise must be present. Never anticipate the music. Make your change of direction very sharp. It was performed as an encore piece by Isadora, probably present in a playful and perhaps flirtatious manner' (Gold 1984: 59).

Duncan's method of inscription allows her to appear ephemeral and weightless. The music sets the narrative of the piece and the method of inscription allows its conditions of reception. The tension between apparent lightness as received by the audience and the technique used by the dancer to create the illusion of this lightness made this dance interesting to Duncan and Gold alike. At the same time it is her embodied space that allows her spectators to perceive her as light and it is her own intervention into her embodied space that creates this method of inscription.

Ann Daly describes this piece as 'lyrical, innocent youth' and argues that such pieces dominated the Duncan legacy (Daly 1995: 62). For Daly, Duncan had achieved her aim of letting the music move the dance and creating a holistic experience: 'Duncan's body was always moving from a single piece, the torso and limbs integrated seemingly' (Daly 1995: 64). The focus is on the discipline of the torso, which allows freedom in the limbs as well as the control of musicality. The awareness by the audience of the use of the solar plexus as the centre of the body, and the originator of movement, allows for the lightness of the perception of the piece.

This is a dialogue between the solar plexus of the spectator and the solar plexus of the dancer. By the use of hands and legs in a light, weightless method, Duncan draws her dancer's attention to the mechanism that allows her to do so – the solar plexus – as the centre of movement, enabling the dancer to sustain that tension. Gold writes: 'the hand, although in a classical ballet position, points with the index finger, as if pointing at a person. This is done with great emphasis' (Gold 1984: 63). Thus this dance is caught in a tension. The dancer's body must mediate two contradictory goals: to make the audience perceive her as light while affirming her own body as present, working through its embodiment to discipline it so that it is perceived as weightless. Contracting deep from her solar plexus and investigating the spatiality of the dancer's body allows it to release into a shared space where it is received as weightless. The dancer is seeking her spectator. She is never alone; there is always someone watching, someone to be acted upon, a shared space to which the body is released. Duncan is aware of the need to pull in the audience members in her choreography of the piece. By pointing at the spectator it is as if she says: you are here. This is a solo which is actually not a solo; it is the dancer moving towards and away from her audience, Isadora Duncan's body spilling into a chorus. Dance for Duncan is always entrenched in a community, the community beyond the dancer performing a solo. Dance is always in search of the spectator, but at the same time it is always able to exceed contemporary communities, in much the same way that she was able to exceed ballet as the only legible method of expression. Duncan's body never ceases to contract and explore its registers; hence it releases different systems of inscription. Let us release into a different phase in Isadora Duncan's life, choreographically and politically.

Revolutionary (choreographed 1921; premiered 1923)

Music: Aleksandr Scriabin, Douze Etudes, Op. 8, No. 12
(www.youtube.com/watch?v=Poic5gNsNSM)

Revolutionary is one of Duncan's later pieces. We must start by noting that the choreographic style is radically different from that of Musical Moment. Musically we see Duncan searching for the beat, accentuating the heaviness of the étude, rather than playfully responding to lyricism in the music as in the earlier Schubert piece. Some of the choreography is against the music, off beat. The work is sombre and severe, and lacks the playful spirit we have seen in the earlier piece discussed above. The dancer uses the floor extensively. She kneels and rises several times throughout the piece, and finishes the dance kneeling. The piece shows the relationship between the solar plexus and its more distant periphery, the floor, providing the dancer with her gravity and heaviness of movement and at the same time revisiting the connection with the audience, which provides the dancer with the impulse for the work – communication. Thus the space of release is extended from the audience to the floor. We should note that in the earlier piece Duncan did not make use of the floor at all; Musical Moment showed the search for ephemerality and lightness of the body by developing a strong core. Revolutionary, however, exposes the technique involved, and shows the indebtedness of the dancer to the floor as grounding her. Revisiting Duncan's rebellion against ballet as a system of movement, which we will recall started with her refusal to stand on her toes and aspire upwards, Duncan here accepts the search for the floor as a legitimate part of her choreography. This is where her stark intervention is at its clearest.

Revolutionary shows a tension between this use of the floor as a gravitational force and an openness of the chest upwards. This openness seems like a cry for help. It is very different from the playful use of hand gestures in Musical Moment. This dance is a plea for a response, for taking part in this danced shriek or angry yell. The dancer uses her hands as if in mourning; she is asking forces larger than herself: *why*? The heaviness of the movement gives the impression that at times it seems that the dancer is tied down by invisible chains. She always manages to break free, start the next movement despite the chains, by releasing into a new space of movement. That space is inhabited by her spectators, manifold sensuous bodies. We may note a technical thread connecting both dances: the use of the hands is central to the choreographic language. The dancer's interaction with the audience, her anger, pain and frustration are communicated through the hands alone.

The dance ends with a fist movement, showing both action and its continuation; there is a feeling that the fist movement has only just started the real action, which will continue when the dance has ended. Again, this fist movement creates a very different use of time and music to that performed in Musical Moment, which utilises circular themes. Here Duncan leaves us with no final statement ending the dance; it remains open-ended.

Nadia Nahumck writes:

> It is truly amazing that in one, brief dance, a single human body can portray the terrible logic of directed anger as an antidote to curdling pain – an explosive finale to restrained endurance. From the first rebellious outcry through trembling emotional intensity to the ultimate defiant thrust of a clenched fist, we are reminded that tyranny begets violence. Evocative power in this dance resonates with the truth found in America's Declaration of Independence – that

when a governing body becomes oppressive 'it is the right of the people to alter or abolish it'.

First presented in 1921, four years after the Russian Revolution, this choreographic gem conveyed the emotional power of tradition-shattering conflict – an unmistakable call to action. (Nahumck 1994)

In reading the dance against the American Declaration of Independence Nahumck removes it from its specific historical context. I proceed to read Revolutionary as articulating in motion the human ability to rebel. Nahumck places an emphasis on the fact that the dance is a call for action, asking the spectators to respond to the dancer's plight and not to remain passive. Ann Daly writes: 'the soloist, representing the archetypical victim of oppression, unshackles her wrists and bangs on the door of the oppressor, finally freeing and empowering herself' (Daly 1995: 186). Daly resolves the tensions discussed above in a moment of freedom and affirmation, showing the heroine as an example of the human ability to overcome oppression. However, as I have shown, the dance alternates between tension with the floor and tension with the audience, and it ends with opening up towards the audience not the floor.

In Duncan's writing, the concept of the third dancer is constantly questioning and moving beyond a known set of meanings. Hence Daly and Nahumck both see this dance simply as an act of self-empowerment, ignoring this constitutive tension between the floor as the base of movement, providing her with constraints from which she is seeking to entangle herself, and the audience member as recipient of the dance. I propose reading this final gesture, of opening the chest and moving the fist in space towards the spectator, as an opening towards further communicative movement, further rebellion. My reading does not suggest a positive finality, showing there has been an act of self-empowerment, and that suffering has been overcome universally; instead I see the central message of this dance as encouraging further dissent from suffering and showing that this dissent is possible. Revolutionary is a request for the audience to contemplate their ability to dissent from oppression. My reading also undermines any reading of the dance as an unequivocal, universal message transmitted to the audience. I argue that reading this dance as choreographically open-ended pushes the onus of interpretation towards the spectator and encourages them to give the dance meaning within their own world. The dance unravels a world-in-becoming for the spectator. It is through human agency, extending the moment of dissent to others, that any conditions such as suffering and deprivation can be amended. The body is but a tool to improve the human condition.

Kimerer Lamothe offers a somewhat different reading of this dance from Daly's:

> Duncan was a revolutionary in more ways than politically, and she was severely chastised, especially by the American public, for her ties to Russia. Thus, it is likely that in this dance she is also revaluing what it means to be a revolutionary and locating that potency in the act and the fact of her dancing rather than in politics per se. It is dancing that Duncan credits with actualizing a conception of life that affirms bodily becoming. It is dancing and not the Bolsheviks who will realize an alternative to the Christian morality that has permeated Western politics. It is dancing that will create not only a new art or a new politics, but a new religion. To be a revolutionary is to dance; to dance is to engage in revolutionary action, to resist the forces of 'inequality, injustice and brutality ... which had made my school impossible'. (Lamothe 2006: 140)

With Lamothe, I argue that the revolutionary spirit of this dance is in the dancing itself, not in the dance's connection to formal institutions or already established political entities with which Duncan engaged throughout her life. Revolutionary is an affirmation of the strong political reading of dance. It is not an affirmation of Russian, communist or American dance but of the transgressive nature of dance as a language. Duncan need not declare herself as 'red' or dance in the nude; her aesthetic revolution is radical in and of itself, in placing her as an equal interlocutor to those who came before her and saw her as an illegible subject.

At the same time, *contra* Lamothe, let us not leave the political frame of interpretation and choose a Christian frame of discourse as Lamothe does in her reading. This dance provides a choreographic interpretation of Duncan as always in movement, while affirming her consistent use of the body as her technical revolution and dissent against ballet. If we are to understand this dance as answering the question 'what does it mean to be revolutionary?', as Lamothe proposes, then the answer should be sought in the language in which Duncan operated, in dance. Her revolution occurs within dance itself, not in the relationship between dance and other systems of signification. Their political power is the ability to affirm a new kind of movement, a new kind of subjectivity, while drawing upon and responding to previous inscriptions on the body. Dance for Duncan is a method of enabling new articulations to be seen and heard. It is a way to affirm the third dancer, dancing unknown systems of signification, who trumps not only the first dancer, representing ballet, but also the second dancer. This reading shows Duncan as revolutionary, opening up shared spaces in which meanings that are yet unknown are for the audience member to decipher. This dance is a celebration of her sic-sensuous, extending her aesthetic revolution towards other sensuous bodies which make of it what they will. It is also an affirmation of the strong reading of political dance, the power of dance to transmit messages independently of words. Let us release further and reflect upon some of the danced responses to Duncan.

Isadora / Duncan: haunting her own boundaries

The reception of Isadora Duncan's revolution is widely debated in dance theory and practice. Peter Kurth starts his biography of Duncan by distancing himself from her image as 'always dancing, always ridiculous, and always with her fatal scarf' (Kurth 2002: x). Mark Franko writes:

> The paradox is that on the one hand, dance history has monumentalised her presence – her charisma, the Duncan myth – which depends on her own irremediable absence. She was unique, historically unrepeatable. On the other hand, her choreography itself, which had become undervalued (or perhaps one might say overpowered by her expressive theory and personal success), recovers Duncan's presence as would the relic of a material signifier with no strings to transcendence attached. (Franko 1995: 4)

Her choreographic intervention discussed thus far probes her spectators to think further; at the same time her revolution is too complex to be effaced by scarves.

In the winter of 1960, the journal *Dance Perspectives* devoted an entire edition to the legacy of Isadora Duncan and Ruth St. Denis, the renowned American choreographer who emphasised orientalism and exoticism through her language of movement, and collaborated with Ted Shawn in the Denishawn school (the alma mater of, among others, Doris Humphrey and Martha Graham, upon whom the next chapter will focus). This edition asks one question only: who was the real founding mother of American modern dance, Isadora Duncan or Ruth St. Denis? Thus this edition of *Dance Perspectives* becomes a fruitful point of reference for seeking seminal moments in the history of modern dance and the performers who created it.

The editorial introduction states that 'both Duncan and St. Denis wanted freedom from convention in order to pursue very positive ideals. And it is from their specific realizations of those ideals that American dance has developed' (Terry 1960a: 4). The similarity of their place within dance history not only refers to their seminal place in dance history but focuses upon the fact that both Duncan and St. Denis were founders in that they were dissenters. At the same time there is something very biased in this discussion from its very beginning, as may be seen here: 'Is there a dancer or choreographer, on Broadway, on educational films or television or, shall we say, in the public eye who is exclusively or even mainly a Duncan dancer?' (Terry 1960a: 25). The journal begins with Duncan's disappearance not presence, questioning the reasons for her lack of existence in American contemporary dance rather than her contribution to it.

As a first step in the discussion, Ruth St. Denis is asked to compare her work to Duncan's. Asking an artist to compare herself or himself to another artist in the question of a true founding moment is a strange move indeed; even more so in a written contribution that seeks to compare the two. Even more so, when, as is the case with Duncan and St. Denis, the artist to whom the speaker compares herself is no longer alive. St. Denis shows some obligatory kindness in her description of her dead counter-exemplar, who cannot respond to this discussion:

> Looking back on both the careers of Isadora and herself, Miss Ruth said: 'when I saw Isadora again (after first seeing her in London in 1900), years later, in California, she inspired me to do something by what she did not do. When she danced to symphonies, she reacted to them and danced when it pleased her to dance. If the music was too fast, she postured. This was all right for her because she was glorious. But for me, watching her, I thought that what I use in such a case would be a symphony of dancers moving to a musical symphony. Thus, my idea for the synchronic orchestra was born.' (Terry 1960b: 27)

Whereas the term 'Isadora' is mobilised to affirm the mythic aura of her rival, St. Denis engages with the aesthetics that Duncan set forth in her dance and critically reacts to them. This is a narration of dissensus articulated through dance. Further, Ruth St. Denis writes:

> America, at the turn of the century, was ill prepared to follow Isadora. Only a few had the discernment to recognize her principles. The same, of course, was true of my work in the early days. But there was a difference between us. When Isadora taught, the most powerful thing students got was spirit, the outpouring of her spirit. In my case, students quite probably missed the purpose of my rituals but by leaning my way, they wound up with routines (the shells of what I stood for) perfectly usable in theatre. (Terry 1960b: 28)

Here St. Denis gives us a clear example of the relationship between technique as inscription and dance. At the same time, she discusses the contribution Duncan made to modern dance history in terms of spirit, not inscription. She constantly writes about her as Isadora, not Duncan. In this she highlights the split between the mythical Isadora and Duncan's embodied presence. This tension is clearly articulated in Charles Weidman's comment: 'we moderns actually revolted against both Isadora and Miss Ruth but we also retained belief in both. For example, Duncan dance is not for me, but Isadora's principles and wonderful spirit are eternal' (Terry 1960b: 40). Weidman illuminates a tension between Duncan dance and Isadora's spirit. This tension is evident in many of the other contributions. The narrations that take Duncan seriously as an aesthetic innovator refer to her as Duncan.[4] Those who argue that her danced innovation is no longer present on stage refer to her as Isadora.[5] Isadora Duncan is a dual figure: there is the real Duncan, who danced and created choreography and whose body was received by other bodies in certain moments in history and by that reception lived on beyond its physical lifetime. The name Isadora carries no ontological weight within it.[6] The name Isadora does not inscribe on a body and does not occupy a space in the world. The name Duncan has written its choreographic revolution upon many bodies, hence is still alive within the world of dance and has a spatial presence upon many bodies. It has been released to a shared embodied space. Those bodies reacted in their own method of inscription and by their contributions keep her very much alive and present in dance history. Their sic-sensuous with her is a lived image of Duncan's inscription upon their body; in their disagreement those spectators keep her presence alive. They legitimated her strong political reading of dance, affirming its independent communicative power. At the same time there is Isadora, the mythic founder, whose grandeur persists over us all, who can be there in spirit without being there in flesh despite the fact that her interventions are first and foremost embodied.

Isadora Duncan unravelled a world in which bodies that were equal responded to her body in a multitude of embodied languages. Her radical intervention was an entanglement of equality and difference; those who dissented from her were able to do so because of her interpretation of a shared space between equal bodies that were able to converse with each other without needing words. Duncan lived in bodies of dancers from the moment she refused to stand on her toes. She is never without a world and never without a body; Isadora Duncan's body has written upon numerous other bodies. The image of Isadora is entangled in scarves, but her spectators know better than to let those scarves hide the radical revolution introduced by Duncan.

Conclusion: 'you were wild once here, don't let them tame you'

I bring back the reader–spectator to Boston, 1922, watching a radically new interpretation of the body, presented in and through a woman who refused to abide by set categories. It was in this performance that Duncan famously said 'you were wild once here, don't let them tame you'. She need not have stated that in words; her performance did so for her. Her performance is the quintessence of the celebration of the strong political reading of dance.

Isadora Duncan starts her aesthetic revolution by dissenting from her ballet teacher. She continues by continually transfiguring her way of thinking about both dance and politics. She never subscribes to a known system of meaning and does not impose an already known linguistic category on her spectator. She invites them to go ahead with her on a journey of questioning. This journey is enabled through her exploration of her own body, the discovery of the solar plexus as the origin of movement and her use of dance as a communicative tool which she had hoped would enable her to create a shared sensation with her spectators. Duncan is more than a revolutionary herself. The embodied space she unravels includes both moments of embodied sharing as well as opportunities to dissent from her in motion. The third dancer, who has the ability to articulate meaning as yet unknown to her, Isadora's moment of intervention (and its use of the solar plexus as communicative) and responses to Duncan in movement which occurred during her life and after her death are all closely intertwined. Isadora Duncan created a shared space of sic-sensuous between her dancers, spectators and herself. Meanings discussed within it are still elaborated. The one incontestable fact, though, is that her own body claimed a space of its own and elaborated that space in a system of inscription.

Duncan allows us to unravel the tensions between the weak reading of political dance, Duncan's shifting associations with various political ideas and institutions, and the strong reading of political dance, her quest to change the way dance is perceived in her day and the way it can be communicated. When we see responses to 'Duncan dance' there is no doubt of the power of her revolution; many people who followed her responded to Duncan dance and created their own moment of dissent, invented their own third dancer and inserted those dancers into the history of dance. Isadora Duncan utilised embodied and choreographic openness that allowed others to respond to her revolution. They do so still. This intervention invites her spectators to go beyond known and agreed upon meanings of political categories set in language.

We may not need to shift away from scarves in order to remember Isadora Duncan as the revolutionary she really was. We may need to shift our attention to the red scarf waved while asking her audience not to be tamed. That scarf, one and the same with her revolutionary body, bringing to the world her unique method of inscription, allows her wild spirit to live on within manifold moving bodies. It is high time for this red scarf to take centre stage when discussing Isadora Duncan, and to allow her revolutionary spirit to be rejuvenated in conversation with the manifold moving bodies which responded to her. One of those interlocutors was another revolutionary, Martha Graham. She enters the argument next.

Notes

1 The only footage remaining of Duncan's actual performance is this very short clip: www.youtube.com/watch?v=oaFZbhbcft0. The chapter will focus on reconstructions of her dances.

2 As Daly notes in *Done into Dance*, Duncan sees the power for social change in the individual rather than the state and yet champions social responsibility, exemplified by her use of the category of 'woman', especially in her essay 'Dancer of the Future' (1902/3; published 1909): 'oh, she is coming, the dancer of the future: the free spirit, who will inhabit the body of new woman; more glorious than any woman that has yet been; more beautiful than the Egyptian, than the Greek, the early Italian, than all women of past centuries – the highest intelligence in the freest body!' It should be noted that she was an early critic of the suffragette movement's focus on the vote and always argued – both in speech and in artistic practice – for a more overarching change to include various categories of class and gender. 'We women can get anything we want in the world without the vote. We doubtless wouldn't keep our names even if we had the right of franchise. We start in life with a man's name – we marry and take another man's name. Now, Isadora belongs to me – Duncan is my father's.' Quoted in an interview with Janet Vale, 14 February 1915, *New York Times*.

3 Duncan's relationship to social-economic reality is especially worthy of comment here. Her biographer Peter Kurth notes that the Duncan household was always on the hunt for money, and she did not complete her schooling as 'no one can learn on an empty stomach'. Nevertheless the Duncan household is described as full of music and poetry (Kurth 2002: 20). In 1905 she founded a school in Gruenwald, which was fully subsidised and aimed at children of all classes; later she extended this enterprise in her sojourn in Russia in 1921 where she dreamed of bringing her art to all and refused to accept money; as she writes in a letter to the People's Commissar of Education, Anatole Vasilief Lunatcharsky: 'I shall never hear of money in exchange for my work … I am sick of bourgeoisie, commercial art. It is sad that I have never been able to give my work to the people for whom it was created. Instead I have been forced to sell my art for five dollars a seat. I want to dance for the masses, for the working people who need my art and have never had the money to come and see me' (Duncan 1929: 24).

4   Hanya Holm: 'for me Isadora was the first modern dancer in Europe. She broke down the conventions and opened new gates. When St. Denis came later, I thought of her as an Oriental, an ethnic dancer. It was Duncan who was really bold, the firebrand. Since then, I have come to realize that what Duncan did was to release the body and its emotions. Her offerings seem spontaneous, the inspiration of the moment' (Terry 1960b: 44). José Limón: 'Although Isadora is my special inspiration, not one day of my thirty years has gone by without one or the other, Duncan or St. Denis, poking me, inspiring me' (Terry 1960b: 47) Conclusion: 'Isadora bequeathed her great spirit, her lyricism and her passion for great music as a dance incentive for those who followed while Miss St. Denis bequeathed a spirituality, a theatricalism and a formal concept of danced drama to her successors' (Terry 1960b: 55). Helen Tamiris: 'In all my teaching ... I go back to Duncan's philosophic point of view. Her dance was expressive of human being, the person in his emotional, philosophic, psychological natures. When I was back in my teens, I saw her last performance in the New York area, in Brooklyn. One moment in particular stunned me. She was dancing the Pathetique. She started on the ground, lying close to the floor and – it took a long time – the only physical action was the very slow movement which carried her from prone to erect with arms outstretched. At the finish, everyone was crying and I was crying too, although it took me too many years to understand what she was doing – that she was living an action or an inner motivation and I was living with her. Years later, while teaching a class, the incident came back to mind. That movement made dance clear to me, that here was dance by and through the human being. Although the content of my own dances was different, this concept, I can say with truthfulness, made possible my career' (Terry 1960b: 42) Tamiris: 'For me, there is only Duncan as a source of historic inspiration but for many others, both Duncan and St. Denis exert their powers' (Terry 1960b: 43) John Butler: 'I lean more towards the theatrical, as Miss St. Denis does, rather than towards the lyrical, which Duncan represented' (Terry 1960b: 50).

5   'Today, I think, Isadora's influence is as strong in America. Form to her was unimportant and she left us no dance disciplines other than children's steps, skips, runs, hops and the like. There are no successors to her, yet the impact is present because Isadora was dedicated to dance and this sense of dedication stimulates our dancers to this day. Isadora symbolized a burning ideal' (Terry 1960b: 44). 'Isadora was unequalled in her spirit of freedom; she was but one person, non-transferable, who travelled on ether to the moon' (Terry 1960b: 44). José Limón: 'In California I read Isadora's *My Life* and I became incandescent with the desire to dance. She was my dance mother, the Dionysian, the drunken spirit of the soul. And today, when I compose, I try to capture that Dionysian ecstasy of Isadora's as she wrote about it in *My Life*' (Terry 1960b: 45). Agnes de Mille: 'Isadora cleared away the rubbish.

She was a gigantic broom. There has never been such a theatre cleaning!'
(Terry 1960a: 25).

6   The interview Duncan gives in 1915, in which she claims her last name is her
    father's but her first name is her own, may help us to expose some misogyny
    and sexism intertwined within her reception; Isadora is sensational, evanes-
    cent, unimportant, as it is her own making; Duncan, her last name, inherited
    from her father, is her legitimate method of intervention into a world of dead
    masters (not mistresses).

3

'The body says what words cannot': Martha Graham, dance and politics

Before Isadora Duncan's untimely exit from the world stage in 1927, she and Martha Graham (11 May 1894–1 April 1991) shared the limelight for a while. After training in 1910 in the Denishawn School of Dancing and Related Arts, mentored by Ruth St. Denis and Ted Shawn, in 1926 Graham founded the Martha Graham School of Contemporary Dance, creating a hub for ongoing embodied conversations and revolutions in American dance. Those revolutions continue, they spill into multiple dancing bodies that are still moving into the future. Martha Graham was a prolific choreographer who drew on manifold sources of inspiration to create 181 dance pieces. Two strands of her work stand out: her 'Americana' choreographies, including, among others, Chronicle (1936), American Document (1938), Letter to the World (1940) and, perhaps most famously, Appalachian Spring (1944), for which Aaron Copeland composed the score. The other choreographic strand that may be identified in her work are her 'Greek', works amongst which are Herodiade (1944), Cave of the Heart (an interpretation of *Medea*) (1946), Night Journey (1947) and Clytemnestra (1958).

This book is written as a tension between contraction and release; my use of these two concepts draws specifically on Graham's interpretation of the concepts on her own body and with many other bodies with whom she conversed. Martha Graham's prolific career illuminated and problematised further political ruptures that were choreographed by Isadora Duncan. Isadora Duncan's body contracts into Graham's, and that in turn releases to create the discipline of modern dance as we know it today.

Graham's career was also interwoven with many political tensions, which differed from the ones Duncan encountered; they set the scene for other choreographic political conversations that will arise on the world stage. Martha Graham gave the world an evolving language with which to think about the world in and through moving bodies. That language was never static and never stable; in line with her interpretation of life and dance (which are always intertwined), this language was entangled in contradictions and tensions. Martha Graham constantly moved beyond the boundaries of her own body and the bodies of her dancers and audience members.

Life is a process of one body releasing into another while always contracting into itself, as Graham knew. This process is not always choreographed and its outcomes are not always intended; some of the most luminous political moments of Graham's career occurred when she unwittingly cast a spotlight on the political contradictions of her life and times. Let us allow her to make her entrance into the argument.

'Movement never lies': Martha Graham's complex politics

Graham's body contracted into itself and released into multiple moving bodies that proceeded to contract and release into other bodies. She unravelled a shared space of dissent and disagreement. The moment in which Isadora Duncan waves a red scarf opens the curtains on a radically different performative world within which Martha Graham takes the stage. Throughout her life Graham created a shared space in which bodies conversed. Those bodies created methods of inscription that responded to her innovative method of inscription. Those meetings between systems of inscription created relationships of sic-sensuous, which in turn were released into engagement with politics carried out by words (for Graham, her dancers and spectators alike).

As an artist whose long life spanned most of the twentieth century and coincided with some of the most dramatic political upheavals of that time, Martha Graham's relationship to politics has been widely discussed in dance studies. It should be noted, however, that this is the first reading of her work within political theory. Together with Isadora Duncan it is difficult, if not impossible, to explain the tension between their centrality in twentieth-century choreographic revolutions and absence within the world of political theory. Interventions in and through the female body are now taking centre stage, after years of being shifted to the wings of political philosophy.

Some analyses in dance studies have focused upon Graham's artistic response to the political events of her time. Helen Thomas quotes from an interview with Graham claiming that there was no intention on her part to choreograph dances of social or political protest (Thomas

1995). Henrietta Bannerman notes that the major concern in Graham's dances from 1926 to 1948 was the individual's struggle for freedom rather than any protest against social or class issues more widely construed (Bannerman 1999). Bannerman goes on to look at the political significance of specific works: 'Chronicle (1936) and Deep Song (1937) reflected anti-Fascist feelings connected with the Spanish civil war and recalled the horror associated with the First World War' (Bannerman 1999: 17). However, McDonagh notes that 'In July, the Spanish civil war began. Though other modern dancers often used political themes, Graham rarely did' (McDonagh 1974: 119). McDonagh goes on to argue that Graham's pre-eminence provided an attraction for those looking for politics in art in the 1930s, 'but where they wanted political commentary, she provided moral parables. Her vision was directed to unlocking the fetters that bound the spirit, not those twisting the social fabric' (McDonagh 1974: 113). Thomas, McDonagh and Bannerman trace in Graham's work the definition of dance as protest in its ability to reiterate opinions and positions articulated in words prior to choreographic intervention. This reading does not seek political positions expressed in the dance itself, independent of politics carried out in words. Thus it is focused theoretically on what has been described throughout the book as the weak reading of political dance. I argue throughout the book for a move away from such a reading of the relationship between dance and politics.

A different strand of discussion on Graham and politics in dance scholarship looks at her public actions and verbal statements. One key event in that narrative is Graham's refusal to perform in the 1936 Berlin Olympics. When Rudolph Laban and the Ministry of Propaganda invited Graham to perform with her company at the Olympics she refused on both ideological and practical grounds; Graham had African-American as well as Jewish dancers in her company and knew that her company as a whole would not be welcome in the Berlin of 1936. At the same time, interpreting this event still draws us away from Graham's dance. Because this depiction of politics and choreography leads us to an understanding of dance as carrying no independent communicative power, I move away from those readings. Contrary to this position I argue that we can find a competing interpretation of politics in Graham's choreography: a method of intervention in public life and a language that can iterate messages independently from spoken language. In this reading I unravel a stage for Graham to act upon using the language she utilised throughout her life, and within which she had claimed equality to those bodies against whom she intervened, including Duncan: dance. In so doing she showed that the body says indeed what words cannot; and the body, always writing upon other bodies, is equal to words as a means of political expression. Let us unravel this realignment of reading her politics to allow her to intervene in a field in which her voice is absent: political theory. I invite the reader–spectator into one space in which a she danced her own sic-sensuous, the State Department-funded tours in which Graham participated.

Martha Graham and State Department-funded tours, 1955–87

During the Cold War, the US State Department funded dance tours to Asia, Africa and Latin America as part of its cultural diplomacy. Those tours were part of the struggle for American cultural and political influence in the (so-called) Third World and aimed to project an image of America as cutting-edge, open and accepting. Eisenhower led the programme, which started in 1954 (Prevots 2001: 8). He is quoted as saying: 'I consider it essential that we take immediate and vigorous action to demonstrate the superiority of the products and cultural values of our system of free enterprise' (Prevots 2001: 22). In the most extensive overarching study of these tours from the perspective of dance, *Dance for Export: Cultural Diplomacy and the Cold War*, Neima Prevots reads the tours in the context of fear of communist ideological and military power and 'its apparent uses in capturing the minds and souls of other countries' (Prevots 2001: 7). After a Congress decision in 1954 to allocate funds to enlist the performing arts in the Cold War, Eisenhower founded the President's Emergency Fund for International Affairs, which funded enterprises sending leading figures in American performing arts abroad. The first dance artist to represent the US on those tours was José Limón, who went to Latin America in 1954 (Prevots 2001).

Martha Graham was one of the most prominent artists to take an active part in this programme. Clare Croft, who has written extensively about dance and cultural diplomacy in the US, argues that Graham was defined as a 'grand lady of dance' in a memo sent in 1974 from Henry Kissinger to Gerald Ford (Croft 2015: 105). But Graham's centrality in American dance predated the State tours. The State Department consequently assumed she had international value, hence was a key figure in the State Department-funded tours. Graham's first tour began in Japan on 23 October 1955.[1] The next stop was Manila, and from there to Indonesia. In a statement in the *Burma Star*, the Burmese prime minister U Nu was quoted as saying: 'Artistes such as Martha Graham can very effectively contribute towards international goodwill and therefore are a potent force for peace' (Prevots 2001: 50). The success of this first tour led the State Department to fund tours which continued till 1987. Prevots notes that Asian audiences responded most powerfully to Night Journey and Cave of the Heart, two of her explicitly 'Greek' works (the former will be discussed in the next section).

The State-funded tours were created to celebrate American exceptionalism and the country's self-perceived superiority. Croft argues persuasively that Graham was a natural choice for the tours due to her American-themed works, which seemed to portray an unequivocally positive image of American freedom (Croft 2015: 109).[2] I intend to focus on the second strand of her works – the Greek strand – which, I argue, posit a clash between what I have called the weak reading and the strong reading of political dance. Graham, like Duncan, drew on ancient Greece in order to mobilise the international power of dance as a language that can transcend boundaries. She drew on the retelling of what she read as universal myths in order to develop her system of inscription. The intersection of the American exceptionalism that funded the performances on State tours, the perception of Greek tragedy as an universal underlying narrative and the extraordinary multiplicity of the psyche and body which inspired Graham's revolution presents a three-tiered sic-sensuous. I now contract into Graham's body to explore the system of inscription that allowed her to perform this sic-sensuous.

Graham's strong reading of political dance

There have been some efforts in dance studies to move away from the focus on intentionality in socially orientated messages and public actions in the reading of dance and politics in Graham's work. In a recent study Victoria Thoms uses the term 'haunting' to examine the relationship between Graham's actual body and its reception, focusing on its unknowability (Thoms 2013). In a powerful study of the political engagement of dancers in New York in the 1950s, Ellen Graff notes that Graham was criticised for being 'too personal and too individual' (Graff 1997: 105), artistic tendencies exemplified in her Greek dance dramas of the 1940s and 1950s. Further, Mark Franko evokes the tension between Graham's verbal statements and the audience reception of her choreographic work: 'Although unequivocal political meaning is not found in Graham's statements, she did court a left-wing audience, and her dances did contain revolutionary fantasies. Her emotional ambiguity, however, was apprehended by the left as political evasiveness' (Franko 1995: 65). Franko shifts from the verbal discourse of the choreographer and her explicit artistic intentions towards the impact of her work on her audiences and their consequent interpretation of politics. We are moved to seek a conflict between politics as articulated in verbal statements and politics as unintentional effects on its audiences, which I show is exactly what Graham accomplished in her choreography.

We begin our interpretation of sic-sensuous in Graham's own philosophy of dance. She writes: 'Throughout time dance has not changed in one essential function. The function of dance is communication. The responsibility that dance fulfil its function belongs to us who are dancing today' (Graham 1937: 50). Dance, to Graham, is never an individualistic enterprise. It is always aimed at conveying a message to someone else. It is intended at an Other, always relational. She writes:

> To understand dance for what it is, it is necessary we know from whence it comes and where it goes. It comes from the depths of man's inner nature, the unconscious, where memory dwells. As such it inhabits the dancer. It goes into the experience of man, the spectator, awakening similar memories. (Graham 1937: 50)

The emphasis in Graham's interpretation of dance is on appealing to the interlocutor, on creating and sustaining a shared embodied space. Intervention always aims towards another body receiving this intervention.

The relationship between aesthetic change and political change is a complex one in Graham's interpretation. She writes: 'great art never ignores human values. There lies its roots (sic). This is why forms change'. (Graham 1937: 50). She elaborates:

> The modern dance, as we know it today, came after the World War. This period following the war demanded forms vital enough for the reborn man to inhabit. Because of the revitalised consciousness came an alteration in movement – the medium of dance, as tone is medium. Out of this dance came a different use of the body as instrument. (Graham 1937: 50)

For Graham, dance is indebted to the political background and cannot be separated from this environment. At the same time, it is always forward-looking, aimed at the spectator who is sitting in the audience, watching and able to share the process that the dancer is undergoing on stage. Graham sees dance as a powerful method of reinterpreting life in a community and the interactions that human beings share with each other, which transcend the immediate setting of the dance concert. For Graham the body always shifts between contracting into its hidden layers, exploring the psyche, and being released into the bodies of her audience members.

In a sentence that seems to directly critique the way politics has been traditionally sought in her work (discussed in the first part of this chapter), Martha Graham writes: 'All of this has nothing to do with propaganda as known and practiced. It only demands the dance be a moment of passion, completely disciplined action, that it communicate participation to the nerves, the skin, the structure of the spectator' (Graham 1937: 51). For Graham, politics in dance must not be reduced to restating our understanding of politics in language. Politics in dance should do something else: create a crystallised instance of complete dedication, a shared space between the communities that have generated it and the ones that receive it. Dorothy Bird, a member of the Graham Company in its first years, wrote:

> Martha said, 'dance has nothing to do with what you can tell in words. It has to do with actions, coloured by deep inarticulate feelings that can only be expressed in movement'. She did not permit a single sentence, neither a subject nor an object, to be considered as a basis for a movement, only verbs and adverbs. (Horosko 2002:48)

Following Graham's writing and this forceful statement, I shift the focus from the narration of choreography to the choreography itself; I shift the focus to the interpretation of dance as a world, or the strong reading of political dance. I invite the reader–spectator to join the moment that Graham unleashed her danced revolution into the world, in one of the first works that exemplify her movement language, Lamentation.

Lamentation (1930)

Music: Zoltán Kodály (www.youtube.com/watch?v=xgf3xgbKYko)

Janet Eilber, former principal dancer in Graham's company and currently the artistic director of the Graham Dance Company, remembers Graham giving her notes to help her lean her torso at exactly the right angle, physically and emotionally: 'it is like you are suspended over the empty womb' (quoted in an interview at Jacob's Pillow Dance Festival, August 2013). Lamentation evokes lack and presence, inhabiting space and withdrawing from it into emptiness, mourning and humanity. The moving body on stage appears nameless, her identity obscure, and the keening, lamenting movements that give the piece its choreographic narrative are without a specific referent. In fact, the dancer, moving inside an immense tube of fabric, loses the most quintessential elements of a dancer: the contours of her own body.

Kimerer Lamothe reads this piece against Duncan's Mother (1924):

> Duncan's 'mother' spills from movement to movement with fluid grace. Her arms reach and curl in unending flow; her torso bends and circles, while her lower body remains fiercely rooted in the earth. The soft folds of the dancer's gown move with her cycles, brushing the air. Graham's figure, rooted to her bench, sheathed in a purple tube of fabric, rocks tightly back and forth. Her movements are stark, percussive. Arms reach and punch, stretch and twist against her torso. The body convulses, doubles over, opaque and articulate in its silence. (Lamothe 2006: 152)

Apart from the theme, mourning and lamentation, these two pieces have very little in common. I join Lamothe in reading this piece as in tension with Duncan, asserting it as a performance of Graham's unique style as a response to Duncan's intervention that, as we have seen, legitimised modern dance. At the same time I read Graham's Lamentation against Duncan's Revolutionary,[3] discussed in the previous chapter.

One of Graham's signature choreographic features was using music in an asymmetrical way. Celebrated Graham dancer Gertrud Schurr writes:

> The measures were not always in counts of four or eight. She introduced us to patterns with new counts, sometimes a slow four as a theme of movement, a three count for a lyrical equality, and a percussive or elevation quality on a two count or even an 'and one' count. This change of accent and counts, mixed rhythms, and uneven measures were additional firsts and Martha used them a great deal. Patterns of ten and five were not unusual. (Horosko 2002: 40)

This use of musicality creates a sense of unexpectedness, a heightened awareness of the movement. I read this use of musicality as Graham's response to Isadora Duncan's musicality. In one of Graham's essays, entitled 'Affirmations' (1936), Graham writes: 'The modern dance of the present time began in America, strangely enough, particularly on the West Coast with Isadora Duncan and Ruth St. Denis' (Armitage 1966: 109). Graham wrote about Duncan in the context of the new-found importance dance had in her day: 'while music of the dance is still transparent and exciting as an element, we still use perennial black velvet of another period as background. They were first used for the dance I believe by Isadora Duncan. She used them, from the same need we have today, to bring focus upon the dance, and she succeeded' (Armitage 1966: 37). Graham placed dance in the limelight independently from other art forms. She reads dance as an expressive medium, able to communicate symbolic messages rather than being a form of entertainment used as divertissement, a piece of movement created solely for aesthetic pleasure. That reading for Graham is indebted to Isadora Duncan. Graham responds to Duncan's revolution in its own language. Duncan's Revolutionary was dark and austere because the music is dark and austere. Graham, however, starts the movement *before* the music. Dance is a method of inscription which writes upon the body independently of any other art form; in this work we see further breaks from music dictating aesthetic. Dance, in Graham's reading, deserves recognition in its own right. In the genealogy of the politics of dance Duncan rebelled against ballet; Graham rebelled against Duncan, and by so doing both affirmed the independent power of dance as a mode of communication. Graham discusses dance with Duncan through the medium that Duncan legitimated, dance.

The moving fist, which ended Duncan's piece, becomes a leaning torso enclosing into itself in Graham's choreography. Graham's lamenting figure is in a never-ending motion of resisting the finalities of her embodied contours. The piece demands utter control of the torso. The dancer holds the audience captive by the movement of her upper body alone. The moving figure succumbs to Graham's language of movement, which becomes one with the dancer's moving body, indiscernible from the tube of fabric enclosing its invisible boundaries. The body moves from inner to outer, from psyche to the invisible boundaries of the body.

Isadora Duncan waved a red scarf and cried: 'you were wild once here, don't let them tame you'. Martha Graham dances the wild, untamed spirit; she uses the demarcation between the fabric and the body in this work as a dual boundary. On the one hand, the tube of fabric effaces the contours of the dancer's body. On the other hand, the use of the fabric as a constraint means the dancer is forced into developing an extraordinary vocabulary of movement while sitting down. Suspended over an empty womb, not only of herself, as a lamenting figure, but of all the bodies with which she is conversing, sharing the physical and emotional journey of mourning and loss, Graham's lamenting figure is a tour de force of a radically new system of inscription. Indeed, Graham shows that she is revolutionary. Duncan's scarf merges into Graham's tube of fabric; but in this case it is in the dance itself, not in words, that Graham performs her revolution.

Graham's engagement with lament and mourning, an underlying theme in her life's work, can be seen in her 'Greek period' in which she interpreted some of the great Greek myths (starting from the 1940s and continuing through the 1950s and 1960s). I move the reader–spectator into another space, created by one of the most celebrated works of that period, Night Journey.

Night Journey (1947)

Music: William Schumann
(www.youtube.com/watch?v=fFNsKeMbW20)

As Henrietta Bannerman, a dance scholar who focuses on Graham's reception of ancient Greece, notes (Bannerman 2010: 259–60), Graham's turn to Greece was very much in the context of her contemporary zeit- geist. Doris Humphrey's dream to create a danced version of the *Oresteia*, which resulted only in Orestes reinterpreted as the Libation Bearers (1933), Anthony Tudor's Lysistrata (1932),The Descent of Hebe (1938) and Judgment of Paris (1938) preceded Graham's 'Greek period' (mainly the 1940s to the 1960s). On Broadway, The Golden Apple (1954), writ- ten by Latouche and Moross, set mythical figures from the Trojan war in a small town in America. Uniquely for her choreographic intervention, Graham's focus was on the individual, and specifically on the feminine individual, the heroines of those tragedies. Here she differs from many of her contemporaries.

Martha Graham's Night Journey, which is her reinterpretation of Sophocles's *Oedipus the King*, does not focus on Oedipus, as the play does, but on Jocasta. It is a reinterpretation of the story from the point of view not of the hero but of what Marni Thomas Wood calls 'Graham's anti heroines' (Wood 2012). Here, again, she continues Duncan's revolu- tion in bringing the female body centre stage, while reading the Western canon against its grain. Premiered in 1947, the piece has been the subject of many debates about the role that feminism, psychoanalysis and, specifi- cally, feminine subjectivity in Greek tragedy plays in Graham's work.[4] This piece was exemplary of Graham's choreographic uniqueness: the ability to present an individual who is always multiple, entrenched in a complex psyche but always referring back to her community, while communicat- ing this complexity to audiences in and through the body. The ability to contest binaries in Graham's choreography is the starting point for the dancing multiple subjectivity that is able to present a new politics in her body while being part of the old order articulated in her words. This dance for Graham is always entrenched in sic-sensuous, engaging two worlds in one: one world in which Jocasta plays second violin to Oedipus and one in which her contradicting embodied psyche takes centre stage.

American dance critic Anna Kisselgoff, writing on Night Journey, commented:

> If one had to choose any fragment of Graham choreography to preserve for
> posterity, the sensational choral passages for these Daughters of the Night

would top the list. Every movement was worked out on Miss Graham's own body as she choreographed the work. To see the angular contractions in which breath is so visibly expelled, or to be stunned by the distortions of the human body for expressive purposes in these passages, is to see choreography that remains incomparable. (Bannerman 2010: 272)

The programme notes for the piece (1967) comment that the chorus of women who know the truth before the Seer speaks it try in vain to divert the prophecy from its cruel conclusion. The chorus are on stage for most of the piece, making it an ensemble tour de force of Graham's choreographic language. Dance theorist Ramsay Burt highlights Graham's interpretation of Greek heroines, and specifically places them as the powerful plot-spinners who have access to knowledge. He writes: 'Jocasta is clearly the strongest role in Night Journey. Unlike Oedipus and Tiresias she is not blind and does not have to become blind in order to gain knowledge' (Burt 1998: 46). At the same time, he acknowledges that there are other characters who have this strength in this piece: the chorus, reinterpreted as 'Daughters of the Night'. Mark Franko, who has written extensively about Graham and politics, reads the chorus as identifying with Jocasta, thus sharing involvement in the action (Franko 2012). The action of the anti-heroine is then distributed between Jocasta's body and the bodies of the Daughters of the Night. Franko quotes Graham as saying that 'there are two areas of action; what may be called the actual and the dream. There is a thread linking the whole and that is the chorus action' (Franko 2012: 107). Graham aims to create a shared space that emerges out of her own body, dancing as Jocasta, through to the Daughters of the Night. Isadora Duncan said she wanted to dance the chorus; Graham, through her use of choreography and narrative structure, created a shared space between herself and the chorus.

I now turn the spotlight onto a series of twelve contractions performed in the midst of the chorus's long choreographic phrase (prior to the tryst between Jocasta and Oedipus), as noted by Kisselgoff. As the chorus performs this series of contractions, we see an extension of the thread of embodied knowledge from Graham's body, dancing Jocasta, onto the bodies of the dancers who perform as Daughters of the Night. But the use of this specific concept in movement is crucial within the ever-changing, ever-evolving Graham vocabulary.

There are two choreographic concepts which accompany the entirety of Graham's career and have a central place within her work: that of the contraction and that of the release. Graham dancer Gertrude Schurr recalls their use as early as in the 1927–28 season (Horosko 2002: 37). In the contraction, the body unfolds into itself, whereas release entails unravelling of the spine outwards and the opening up of the body towards its environment. In the action of contraction the dancer explores the density of her own corporeality, in her inner being, while exhaling, whereas in the release the dancer places herself in her spatial setting and locates her body within its surroundings, while inhaling. In the action of release the torso opens towards the world – the dancer inhales and utilises the movement to explore the spatiality of the stage and the body, as well as other bodies with which she is always conversing. These two actions are based not only on the body's anatomy but also on the primordial action of breathing, reflecting the tension between inhaling, taking air from one's surroundings, and exhaling, letting the air go to one's environment. This shift draws on the materiality of the body but enables the dancer to mould it through disciplined action, and then communicate that action to other material bodies. The duality of this conceptual tension allows the Graham dancer to explore and delve deeper into her material subjectivity. Dance theorist Kimerer Lamothe, who has written extensively on Graham and Duncan, argues that contraction and release relate to Graham's reading of Nietzsche, which informed her aesthetics: 'they (contraction and release) are a way of "doing an I"' (Lamothe 2006: 82); they are part of the project of bringing movement back to life and life back to movement, and reinterpreting dance as a method of communication independent of words; affirming dance as a world.

Drawing on the analysis above, it may seem at first sight that the release is the more communicative action of the two; it is that action that returns the dancer back to awareness of her surroundings and other dancers around her. However, the foundational philosophy underlying Graham's technique shows that the contraction was just as vital for Graham as a communicative tool. As Graham dancer Alice Halpern writes, 'The contraction not only fosters control of the torso and strengthens the abdominal area, it is also an inherently dramatic movement, a means to the expression of the inner landscape' (Halpern 1991: 23). Copeland notes that 'Graham's contraction [also] serves to generate an involuntary muscular response in the perceiver, thereby uniting the spectator and the dancer in a shared kinaesthetic experience' (Copeland 2004: 141). The contraction, although seemingly inward looking, is communicative in its unravelling of a space for the spectator in which she shares the sensation experienced by the dancer. It is grounded in the exhalation, returning air into the physical space the dancer inhabits. Hence it is Graham's way to generate collective feeling, a shared state of bringing the internal into external expression through movement and for emotion to be experienced by dancer and spectator.

The chorus is assigned the role of drawing the audience into the piece, making them actively engage in the narrative through the use of contraction. As the contraction draws the body of the dancer and the body of spectator together, it allows further extension of the dialogue between Jocasta and the chorus, the Daughters of the Night, as discussed above. But beyond that moment of sharing, by using contractions Graham's aim is that the audience also becomes part of Jocasta's psyche, thus expanding the threads of those who share this position of privilege with regards to knowing the narrative. Night Journey is grounded in creating spaces of embodied sharing; between the protagonist and the chorus and between the dancers on stage and the audience. The use of contraction and its interpretation arose from Graham's own body and the bodies of her female dancers. The contraction starts from the vagina. Graham's movement vocabulary and choreography start from her female body, which she elucidates and illuminates, allowing others to share in that process. The use of contractions in Graham vocabulary, then, gains further centrality when read in this context; through the extensive disciplining of the torso in contractions, Graham opens up a shared space between the spectator and the dancer. Jocasta, the anti-heroine who retells the story of Oedipus the king, starts the retelling from the core of her femininity; that retelling extends to other women sharing the stage with her, and then extends into the audience. The body is saying what words cannot; it is retelling a canonical story while constantly questioning the boundaries between inner and outer, psyche and body, and one body and another.

We start watching Martha Graham's choreographic journey from her lamenting figure, contesting her own embodied boundaries though constantly releasing into the bodies with whom she converses. We continue this journey with a shared embodied space, enabled by a specific reading of the contraction, between Jocasta, affirming the centrality of the woman protagonist in Oedipus the King, the Chorus, and the members of the audience. The empty womb spills into an array of female bodies, contracting into themselves and conversing with each other, expressing their individual voices. The boundaries of this shared embodied space are construed by the ever-deepening, ever-changing contraction. They are never stable. Martha Graham and her interlocutors move beyond boundaries on multiple registers.

Martha Graham provoked much disagreement in her unique interpretation, outlined above. Kirstein wrote in the *New Republic*: 'her jumps are jolts; her walk, limps and staggers; her runs, heavy blind impulsive gallops; her bends, sways. Her idiom of motion has little of the aerial in it, but there's a lot of rolling on the floor' (McDonagh 1974: 65). Graham never tried to be a crowd pleaser; her dances were not aimed at cheering up spirits, or creating an enjoyable evening. Indeed, influential dance writer Edwin Denby writes: 'I find watching her not a balm for the spirit, but certainly a very great pleasure for the intelligence' (Denby 1986: 128). Graham's work was unsettling; it was definitely not considered beautiful in the simple sense of the word. Elsewhere Denby writes:

> It isn't often I've seen in the lobby in the intermission so animated discussion of a ballet as it was after Martha Graham's new Deaths and Entrances. The piece is a harsh one: it has neither a touching story, nor a harmonious development, nor wit and charm to help it along. But at both its recent performances it held the audience spellbound. (Denby 1986: 109)

Graham knew very well how to present and perform a sic-sensuous, a presentation of an aesthetic not always considered beautiful experienced between two sensing bodies.

Slightly more light-hearted but no less critical receptions of Graham are quoted in Copeland's book on Merce Cunningham, Graham dancer turned into revolutionary in his own right. In reference to titles in characters in her Dark Meadow, such as One who Seeks, He who Summons, The One who Speaks, Copeland terms Graham herself: 'she whose head ached from allegory' (Copeland 2004: 26). In perhaps one of the most famous lines of criticism of her work, echoing the sharp, angular movement that became her signature, Stark Young responded to an invitation to see a Graham performance: 'must I go? I'm so afraid she's going to give birth to a cube on stage' (Copeland 2004: 26). Graham's sic-sensuous, her ability to elicit strong responses drawing solely on the body, allowed her to penetrate other political worlds, as I show next.

'In my beginning is my end': from the universal body to universal dissent

The argument in this chapter started from Graham's body lamenting alone on stage; it then proceeded to spill into the body of Jocasta, conversing with the Daughters of the Night, the chorus in her Night Journey. This progression allows us to contract further into Martha Graham's unique sic-sensuous.

The first layer of the sic-sensuous that we see in Graham's work emerges from her interpretation of dance as a method of communication that transcends borders and communities demarcated by verbal language, and the American exceptionalism policy that funded her tours abroad. During the 1955–56 tours Graham was asked: 'Why are there no dances in your company in which the subject is universal brotherhood?' To which she replied, 'There are no dances in my company in which that is not the subject. I could not do a single step if I did not believe in brotherhood. But I am not a propagandist. I don't need to make dances that say they are about brotherhood. All my dances are' (Prevots 2001: 53). Graham's universalist narrative is exemplified in her Greek works, which, as we have seen, were particularly popular within the context of the State-funded tours. The celebration of American superiority stands in sharp contradiction to Graham's strong reading of politics as performed in Night Journey. As an example of Graham's philosophy of choreography, her dance shows the inner contradictions communicated to the spectators through various choreographic mechanisms. It is hardly possible to perform a singular narrative of American superiority in a dance that shows the complexity of humanity and communicates this complexity beyond boundaries.

At the same time, Graham's interpretation of the universal power of dance is not without problems and inner contradictions. Clare Croft argues that Graham placed a white female body against a literal or figurative backdrop of multiracial performers (Croft 2015: 111). Graham dancer and scholar Ellen Graff expands on this point: 'Graham's universal body was almost certainly assumed to be a white Protestant body that somehow could subsume every other identity' (Graff 1997: 130). Presenting Graham's body as a source of the universal language of movement erases the social, racial and economic inequalities in which she intervenes. The white, female, middle-class body is presented as the universal body and those who do not relate to it are marginalised. John Martin's writing on Graham and Pearl Primus, discussed in Chapter 1, shows us that this presentation was indeed dangerously successful. The white heteronormative body is presented centre stage as universal. Other bodies can merely but respond to it. At the same time, let us revisit the argument presented in Chapter 1: the body is not universal but the body is able to intervene universally. Drawing on Hannah Arendt's argument that underlying equality enables the communication of difference, I reread Graham's attempt at universalism as exposing the politics of intervention from unique bodies posed against her own. This unique and singular moment reveals Graham's intent to create shared spaces of sensation actually traversing geopolitical boundaries in dissent rather than creating conformity to her own body.

Martha Graham cannot choreograph the responses to her choreography; those are as diverse and manifold as the registers of the dancing psyche she focused on throughout her life. Graham contracts into her own body. However, that contraction releases dissent in other bodies that respond to it. Universalism in intention becomes a singularly located moment of disagreement that is never beyond a particular space-time. That space-time, always located in a moving body, is in and of itself a harsh critique of a singular narrative of universalism. The failures of Martha Graham's universalist narratives become the success of the sic-sensuous lying at the heart of her choreography, championing the complexity of the individual embodied psyche. I invite the reader–spectator to share one such moment of dissent in one particular performance.

Clare Croft quotes Graham Company artistic director Janet Eilber reflecting on her memories of performing in another Graham signature piece, Diversion of Angels (premiered 1948). Eilber recalls the performance setting, which largely comprised a military audience: 'If you fall off stage, usually you run into a wall eventually. But there were no walls there [that night]. The theatre was open to the alleys that were there beside the theatre, and there were just storefront gates across them ... the gates were filled with faces of people who lived in the alleys [who were] watching us' (Croft 2015: 136).

The piece ends with Eilber's danced character opening her chest and arms towards the audience, in this case the uninvited audience members who watched from the sides of the stage. This moment of shared sensation between Eilber and the uninvited recipients of her movement shows another level of Graham's sic-sensuous. This sic-sensuous occurs between the audience as demarcated by 'legitimate' ticket holders and those uninvited guests who indulge in the shared sensation nonetheless. This clash unravels inequality experienced outside the theatre, between privileged and underprivileged bodies, those deemed worthless and not allowed to be formal spectators, and their improvised experience of spectatorship in which they are equal to those who exclude them. This clash shows both those characteristics that make bodies unequal and that shared capacity that allows bodies to relate to each other beyond those differences. This is not an appeal to the universal body as a source of communication that allows a plot to unravel and knowledge to be shared. This performance exemplifies the universal capacity to dissent through the body as a mechanism to elicit intervention in a way that transgresses physical and non-physical boundaries. Further, this moment of transgression shows the differences between various bodies, as well as their equality in response to each other. The presentation of a narrative of universalism ends in a moment of reception that shows that the most universal feature about human bodies is their resistance to final boundaries. Graham's uninvited audience members, in creating a shared embodied space with Eilber, not only resist the boundaries set by the conception of the theatre, they resist being deemed as unequal by those, the privileged, invited audience members. Graham's dance drew on the complexities of the human psyche and body. In so doing it unravelled further possibilities for transgression, which are always located in a moving body responding to her choreographed bodies in motion on stage.

In her diaries, which contain elaborate choreographic notes on the sources that she read for inspiration (from Plato to T. S. Eliot, Nietzsche and many more) and explicit stage directions, Graham writes (Graham 1973: 302):

> People say –
> How did you begin?
> Well – that is the question –
> And who knows –
> *Not I*[5]–
> How does it all begin?
> I suppose it never begins, it just continues –
> Life –
> Generations –
> Dancing

Graham's choreography enabled a sic-sensuous between the body, which is able to create shared spaces through breathing together, the most primordial action that underpins our lives as human beings, and systems that deem some bodies superior to others. In her notes for one of her works, Episodes 1, Graham rewrites a T. S. Eliot line from his poem *Four Quartets: in the beginning is my end* turns into *in my end is my beginning*. Susan Jones provides a profound literary analysis of this move (Jones 2009, Jones 2013); here, however, I focus on the political significance of this rephrasing. The end of the presentation of a coherent narrative through the weak reading of Graham's political dance was the beginning of the strong reading of political dance as an interruptive language that entails acts of writing between two sensuous bodies. In Martha Graham's end was her beginning. There was nothing cohesive or singular about her interpretation of dance. Martha Graham's body existed in performance, but at the end of the performance her body was carried by multiple bodies who responded to her dedicated acts of light. Her body becomes luminous in the reception of other bodies responding to it, running towards an angel diverting into the audience. Isadora Duncan started the revolution. Martha Graham celebrated it. The flaws in her reception were her biggest success; those ruptures and inconsistencies unleashed numerous systems of inscription, which have given us modern dance as we know it today, in the US and beyond. All dancing names and all moving bodies find a trajectory in Martha. From Merce Cunningham to Pina Bausch, no one can escape the Grand Lady of dance asking them how it all begins. She knew it is not for her to answer. The only way to understand dance is to turn the spotlight on those who are there to continue the movement after the performance ends. Performance is ephemeral, and a dancer's life is entangled in contradictions and hesitations, but dance never really starts. It is always a continuation to another dance. It is always the count starting after the 'one' count. The errors and misreceptions are as essential a part of Graham's politics as her intended and articulated reading of dance.

Many people unconnected with dance for stage as performed in contexts such as the ones discussed in my reading of Duncan and Graham understood very well its immense power to intervene in political configurations in and through the body while challenging the boundaries of what is deemed acceptable and beautiful. I now invite the reader–spectator to turn to an instance in which dance was used as a means of communication when words were not allowed, and where it played with the boundaries of equality and inequality in a completely different setting: the gold mines of South Africa.

Notes

1   Victoria Thoms notes that Graham subtly influenced the panel to allow her to go on tour (Thoms 2013).
2   Croft bases her analysis on the contradictions between those explicit messages (articulated, among other ways, by reading onstage the Gettysburg Address and the Emancipation Proclamation) and the choreography of Phaedra and Night Journey, in particular, which exemplify the tensions between freedom and un-freedom (Croft 2015).
3   Ann Daly also sees choreographic resemblances between the two pieces in her *Done into Dance*.
4   Croft provides a reading of this piece as what she terms a 'diva stance', a hybrid gender identity, portraying both female sexuality and modes of masculinity (Croft 2015). Ramsay Burt argues that 'Night Journey subversively re-appropriates a canonical text in order to interrogate the psychological construction of feminine subjectivity through the discourse of psychoanalytical theory' (Burt, 1998: 50). Marni Thomas Wood, who performed in this piece and reconstructed it, writes about Jocasta: 'she surrenders to the vulnerability of being a woman, her downfall growing out of her endeavours to define herself in the consummate role of wife/mother/lover queen' (Wood 2012).
5   My emphasis.

4

'I want to tell them how I feel and how black people feel': gumboot dance in South Africa

Isadora Duncan's rebelling body, dancing the chorus, was released into Martha Graham's contracting chorus. But Duncan and Graham were not the first to mobilise choruses and their transgressive potential. I invite the reader–spectator to watch gumboot dance in South Africa, which, as we will see, utilised many elements performed by Graham and Duncan in a radically different context. The body is able to intervene universally; and it does so beyond theatrical performances. I release the intervention illuminated in the choreography of Martha Graham into conditions in which speech was rendered impossible by economic, legal and political frameworks.

Gumboot dance developed as a method of communication within systems of racial segregation in which speech was prohibited. Verbal communication was not allowed in the gold mines, nor were black South Africans allowed to enter the public sphere, hence their opinions and voices were silenced. I argue that the development of gumboot dance allowed for two parallel processes: firstly, the African mining community developed a non-verbal voice; and second, that voice was then heard by those who established systems of racial segregation that perceived that mining community as unequal. In this way, dance as a method of communication transcended legal and political systems that deemed some members of the body politic inferior and prohibited those members from speaking. At the same time, this chapter looks at how gumboot dance was received in conditions of severe racial inequality. The reception of this form of dance is a method of disciplining and policing the black voice, reinstating the systems of inequality it had transgressed. Thus the chapter carefully examines the relationship between intervention and inscription. It shows that moments of sic-sensuous have not always been mobilised as a force for the good. Let us contract into the dark setting of the South African gold mines and allow the performance of gumboot dance to commence.

'But they have not heard us say it': the origin, history and aesthetics of gumboot dance[1]

South Africa's political history is marred by a narrative of racial segregation, which led to the development of the apartheid regime (1948–94). Racial segregation was organised around legal and political structures that disabled communication between the white and the black population. Gumboot dance originated in the gold mines of South Africa, where working conditions were hard and talking was forbidden (Dixon 1998). On 17 February 1920, the 2,000 workers in the Cason compound at the massive ERPM complex went out on strike. Within days, workers struck on every major mine and thirty-one compounds across the reef. By 28 February, when the strike finally ended, some 71,000 workers had taken part in the stoppage, with over 30,000 being out on six consecutive days, and a further 25,561 on the seventh (Breckenridge 1998). On 7 December David Nkosi, a Mozambican migrant in the Simmer and Jack compound, sent a letter to his compatriots in the coal mines in Witbank:

> To all the Witbank people, we inform you about the matter we have started ... It is very good that all the Mines must do the same. Wake up the people, we must speak for ourselves without talking we will never get anything from the white people ... You know that the matter is good when there are a lot of people talking about it you must go round and spread the news. We have also sent the message to Randfontein we have started here and called the white man, you must do the same. (Breckenridge 1998: 79)

Further, Matthew Butelezi, one of the workers from the Comet compound, wrote to Abantu Batho about the strike. 'When we went out from underground we met the boys from the New Comet outside the Compound ... The white man in charge of the E. R. P. Mines came and he said "What is it? What do you want to do here?" The boys said "We want to speak for ourselves"' (Breckenridge 1998: 81). Economic exploitation was inextricably linked to the lack of a public sphere and the silencing of voices of black miners. The mines were prone to flooding and hence the miners wore wellington boots, known as gumboots. Those boots, designed to sustain the miners in highly dangerous and volatile working conditions and enable them continue working within this harsh environment, were the beginning of the development of a non-verbal communication system in the mines.

Dixon writes:

> in the dank, dark shafts, workers learned to send messages to each other by slapping on their boots ... faced by this repressive regime, workers adapted traditional dances and rhythms to the only instruments available: their boots and bodies. The songs that were sung to go with the frenetic movements dealt with working-class life – drinking, love, family, low wages and mean bosses. (Dixon 1998)

I utilise the conceptual framework offered here to analyse gumboot dance as a political language. Gumboot dance arose from conditions in which some human beings were treated as unequal and were not allowed to speak and be heard. Moreover, these conditions placed their lives in constant danger for the benefit of another group of the population. Gumboot dance is a method of communication that in its very performance punctures the structures that render its performers as non-legible and non-legitimate speakers. Thus it is transgressive, creating tears in the legal–political structures that consolidate inequality, and doing so in and with the body. It is an enunciation of the strong reading of political dance in conditions in which the weak reading of political dance is impossible. However, as this chapter shows, gumboot dance carries far more complex histories, making it an important intervention into the reading of political dance. Gumboot dancers unravel a significant moment of sic-sensuous. Insights into the interplay of the various sources of influence upon the choreographic texture of gumboot dance are revealed by listening to this rare quotation from an early gumboot dancer, Johnny Hedebe: 'In 1896, subsequent to watching white men tap dancing and clapping their hands, the amaBaca decided to make a dance of *their own*.[2] They called it the gumboot dance. The dance was a rhythmically performed act of dancing, clapping hands and slapping the calves – the calf muscles being protected by the rubber gumboots' (Muller 2008: 138).

There are contradictory accounts about the exact historical origin of gumboot dance. In one theory the dance originated around the gold mines and later spread to Durban (Muller and Fargion 1999). Carol Muller and fellow ethnomusicology student Janet Topp Fargion learned gumboot dancing from gumboot musician and dancer Blanket Mkhize and performed with him until 1985 and again in the early 1990s. This chapter utilises much of their research and insights, which combines first-hand experience with ethnomusicological knowledge. Muller claims, 'the environment most crucial to the formation of Gumboot was the peculiar

social space of the gold mine in and around the city of Johannesburg'
(Fargion 1998). Miners were organised into groups of workers, each with
a black 'boss-boy' who was answerable to the white miner. This triadic
relationship produced tensions and conflicts in loyalty for the boss-boy
(Muller and Fargion 1999). Isicathulo or gumboot dance was developed
around missions stations in KwaZulu Natal with the introduction of
footgear to African people by missionaries in the late nineteenth century, later changed into gumboot when they were purchased for work
purposes (Muller and Fargion 1999). Thus gumboot dance was deeply
entrenched in the living conditions of the miners from its rural inception
and beyond. Fargion argues that many sequences also make reference to
urban life experience:

> The sequence called Isihamba na Dali (Go with your darling/girlfriend) is a
> reference to the fact that, as it was explained by the dancers, it was easier to
> walk along the street with a woman because two men walking together were
> instantly suspicious. As far as the authorities were concerned they could be up
> to no good. (Muller and Fargion 1999: 109)

This suspicion by the authorities together with letter quoted at the beginning of the chapter around the miners' strike of 1920 illuminate the fear
that the white bosses felt of organisation among the black miners, as well
as their attempt to take total control over their workers' lives. Dancers
releasing into bodies of their fellow miners signalled immediate danger
to those who deemed them unequal.

Many dance sequences make direct reference to mining locations
such as Germiston, Benoni, Johannesburg, Amaphoyisa, Abelungu and
to urban experience. For example, Good Morning Baas, a reference to
white people, sets the dancers on their knees in a praying position; the
spatial relationship in the dance replicates relationships of authority in
the non-danced world. Some sequences are a direct reference to mining
experience, such as Danger! Muller and Fargion point out that the two
names of a single dance routine, Amaphysa! Amablekjek!, alerted men
to the presence of two kinds of police in the mines (Muller and Fargion
1999). Gumboot dance was both entrenched in the relationship between
the white bosses and the black miners and subverted it. From early on,
gumboot dance was patronised by the white bosses as a means of boost-
ing morale among the workers and thereby illuminating their control
over the miners' lives. The white bosses encouraged the formation of
teams which would rehearse and compete in performance with teams
from other compounds. The use of this dance as a tourist attraction has

also led to the understanding, in some areas, of the dance as manipulated by white people (Muller and Fargion 1999).

From its inception and throughout its performance history the dance exhibited the disciplining of the African population by the white population in South Africa. Gumboot dance, then, not only imitated and performed the politics of inequality that circumscribed the miners' lives, but it also helped to sustain the miners as inferior. At the same time, the dance subverted the systems of inequality that set the scene for its inception by denying them a voice. In this way gumboot dance represented that which was not to be discussed, and created a shared symbolic system between those who were not allowed to speak.

Fargion and Muller note that gumboot dance enabled people to establish personal networks, as it brought people together from the same rural areas (Muller; and Fargion 1999). It was, first and foremost, a method of communication and a sharing of embodied knowledge in extraordinarily difficult living conditions. The physical boundary that was there to protect the body in precarious working conditions – the gumboots – also allowed the miners to create a shield against the politics that rendered them unequal bodies by generating an embodied language. I contract further into the bodies of the dancers as the reader–spectator is invited to watch two performances of gumboot dance. The reader–spectator here is placed in a different location to the white bosses, who were not part of the symbolic system developed by the miners and yet their control of their lives was manifested in the system of inscription as well as its reception. The dance presents a critical intersection between oppression and the means to transcend it; both inequality and equality. Gumboot dance illuminates what I read as the strong reading of political dance or the independent political power of dance. Let us contract further, from the dark cold mines into the moving and moved bodies of the gumboot dancers.

'We need to speak for ourselves': choreographic analysis of gumboot dance

Gumboot dancers in Cape Town (2007) (www.youtube.com/watch?v=iSgFAGomtac)

This first example is a bootleg video shot probably by a tourist of an apparent busking or a spontaneous street performance. The only information supplied is 'these gumboot dancers were brilliant'. The end of the video shows an all-white audience sitting in a coffee shop.

The dance starts – and finishes – with a line of dancers moving together. One moving body releases into another. The dancers are mostly bent over, leaning towards their boots. They either stomp, clap or hit their boots. The concept of body music becomes clear through their performance. The dancers' posture directly embodies mining actions. Thus the primary – and perhaps focal – characteristic to be noted is the use of space in a dual way: first, the dancers are in a long line (they are all equal to each other in this line); and second, they are mostly bent, subsumed. The spatial demarcation that placed them in the mines is repeated within the choreographic language itself. The dancers' body language shows their acceptance of someone else organising their space. It should be noted here that the dancers perform in front of moving traffic, making themselves vulnerable in a dangerous environment. Spatial control – the dance being performed in dangerous locations – is unwittingly transferred from the dance's point of origin, the mine, to its current performance location.

I contract further to problematise the spatial organisation of the dancers. First, throughout the clip (at 1:32, after a solo which will be discussed next; 1:47; 2:01; 2:08; 2:15) the entire line of dancers moves together. They either shift forward, or stand up, or both. The line of dancers appropriates space; moreover, this space, as the reader–spectator knows, has not been assigned to them. One quintessential element of mining lives was the restricted space that miners occupied, and the harsh living conditions that arose out of this spatial configuration. In this clip we see gumboot dancers transgressing this spatial configuration. The dancers appropriate – or occupy – a space that is not theirs to inhabit. In these moments subversion of authority occurs. The dancers do not accept their subsumed spatial location, and moreover resent that spatial location as a whole rather than as dissenting individuals.

At the same time, this spatial organisation is also broken by a subtle interplay between solos, or 'singles', and unison (discussed in the last section); this is the second characteristic of the choreography to be acknowledged here (moments at 0:30; 0:37; 0:55; 1:21; 1:28; 2:08). The living conditions of the miners-turned-dancers led to a strong emphasis on unison dancing. At the same time, this unison often breaks in rapid changes: 'The dancers are expected to respond quickly, without hesitation, regardless of what the leader commands. Precision of movement – starting and ending on the same beat – is crucial to effecting a powerful performance' (Muller and Fargion 1999: 90). Gumboot dance is characterised by shifts from one sequence of movement to another, encouraged by calls from the leader, hence in its performance it shows the discipline within the group. Further, the dance performance is shaped by a series of commands, paralleling the development of fankalo, meaning 'like this', a language the whites invented when speaking to the black workers. Fankalo was developed by the southern African mining companies, and composed of corrupted elements of the Nguni languages, English and Afrikaans. It is a language black miners never spoke among themselves.

Highly competitive solo performances, called 'singles', demonstrating improvisatory skills, interrupt unison sequences in gumboot dance (Muller and Fargion 1999). The soloists are thrown money by the spectator. The better the solo, the more money is thrown at the performer. The unison dance of the chorus-like line is broken into a singular body contracting into itself. The reader–spectator may be reminded of Arendt's statement emphasising the tension between individuality and equality: because human beings are equal, they are able to communicate with each other. Because they are different, they have ideas to share. Because gumboot dancers are equal, they are able to break out of the line and communicate this break to their fellow dancers who stop the unison movement. Because they are different, they have those different solos to perform.

Muzaffer Ozgubulut discusses gumboot dance as a kind of body music, which is a sequence of music that begins with making sounds on the body (Ozgubulut 2012). He also comments on the process of learning body music that is directed by a 'leader' and specifically the process of echoing movement and sound. By consolidating the relationship between the leader and dancer, and through the use of mirroring and echoing as a choreographic device, the dance retains an open-ended choreographic structure that constantly invites other dancers to join. This tension between unison and a leader, and the process of echoing, enables moments of shared embodied space which are structured as part of the dance. The contraction into a single moving body is always echoed into releasing into other sensuous bodies. The use of body music allows the dance to sustain this tension without requiring words.

This characteristic is also a bridge between the audience and the performers. The recipients of the dance are essentially participatory; they allow for a dialogue between the dancers and spectators. When they clap the dancers along, they enter into the movement of the dancers (which significantly draws on clapping). This dialogue invites more people to participate in the dance through creating a shared embodied space in which participants communicate on equal grounds. The movement releases towards an expanding line of gumboot dancers.

Those solos are improvisatory and break the rhythm and structure of the unison movement, which in turn responds to them. This is a vivid example of the tension between contraction into a single body and release into the dancing line, moving as one. Within the dance – which is read here as a disruption in itself – these are moments of interruption in which the singular dancer intrudes on the movement of the line. The unison subverts the systems that do not allow it to be heard; the solo subverts the unison. In this context it is also important to highlight the fact that two of the moments in which the line moves and stands up (at 0:37; 1:28) follow those solos. It is clear that the collective reorganisation of space is a response to the individual, more spontaneous, intervention. While the dancers shout commands to each other throughout, the movement precedes the language. The body moves first, then comes the command. Thus the solos have a dual interruptive force; firstly in terms of spatial organisation and secondly within the movement itself.

The tension between contraction and release occurs in other registers of the dance. Whereas the movement in the clip is indeed confined spatially, rhythmically it is, in fact, highly flexible. The rhythm of the dance changes constantly; it is impossible to count here the number of different rhythms that the dancers create in this short sequence. Contraction into a specific musical phrase swiftly releases into a different one. Thus even without noting the re-appropriation of space, discussed above, the use of musicality in a shifting, fluid manner is transgressive in and of itself. Bearing in mind the historical context of the development of the dance, this is significant for two reasons: not only does it represent resentment at being confined spatially (as if the dancers are saying: you may conscribe our use of place, but you cannot conscribe our use of rhythm); also, the constant change of rhythm (and its use in creating changing responses from the dancers) means that the dancers are always attentive to individual rhythmical changes. The embodied space shared by the dancers is always moulded by interruptions from the members of the line, which break away from it musically and spatially. There is a dual release: into space and within the rhythms employed as part of the dance.

The presentation of this musical characteristic in perfectly co-ordinated musical shifts is testimony to the dancers' ability to listen and respond to individual changes of pulse. The individual body is always entrenched in its community of other sensuous bodies.

I invite the reader–spectator to shift to yet another register of tension between contraction and release. The use of clapping and stomping draws the audience into the dance. Moreover, the heavy choreographic reliance on these elements seems not just a necessary outcome of the space in which this dance originated. It is also a method of constantly opening up the dance to more participants, who respond through the leader–follower structure within the dance. By making central an element which in and of itself encourages participation, the dance remains constantly open to new participants, encouraging them to be equal in that moment of clapping. The result is a chorus that is always releasing into further space.

I read the line of gumboot dancers and those soloists who break away from that line against Isadora Duncan, who tried to dance the chorus, and Martha Graham as Jocasta sharing her danced, entangled psyche with the chorus of Daughters of the Night. We see that the chorus as a spatial organisation, a group of dancers sharing embodied space, is crucial for creating a strong reading of political dance. This feature should not be read within the context of Western choreographic tradition alone; the use of the chorus as a unison body in motion which expresses the individuality of its members is a narrative that underlies all the case studies discussed thus far. At the same time, in all these discussions I focus on the interruptive horizons that the chorus opens up rather than the homogenising features of its movement. All these choruses opened up further spheres of contestation and intervention, allowing more voices to join them. Isadora Duncan opened up further spaces for dissent in movement by dancing the chorus; Martha Graham allowed the complexity of psychic life to unravel by dividing the action between Jocasta and the Chorus, by opening up spaces for interruption in the narrative of Night Journey and through the use of the contraction as a choreographic mechanism for shared embodiment. Here, we see the line of gumboot dancers constantly interrupted by soloists who break away from its unison movement, performing in their individual style and inserting their language into the choreography as a whole. Using the leader–group interaction that underpins body music opens up this sphere of contestation further. In all these instances the chorus allows for the unfolding of a shared embodied space of dissent. The reader–spectator is invited to a different performance of gumboot dance in order to delve further into the choreographic uniqueness of this dance. More gumboot dancers are hence invited into the conceptual limelight.

Waterford Kamhlaba (2013)

(www.youtube.com/watch?v=fYYYymWvhAI)

Although this clip looks significantly more choreographed than the previous one, and includes dancers from both genders (as opposed to the first clip, which was all male, much like the miners who created this dance), it contains similar elements to the ones discussed thus far: punctuation of unison with solos ('singles'), changing spatial configuration, changing rhythms (showing the multiplicity of influences upon the dance) and of course the constant stomping, clapping and use of footwear in various percussive elements. This dance also draws upon a basic embodied position explicitly referring to the action of mining, just like the first clip discussed. The discussion of this clip will focus on its unique musicality. There are two moments where I shall pause – they occur at 1:18 and 1:51 in the clip – where a 'single', a solo, shifts the groups' movement and rhythm into a new sequence. These interruptions then become part of the groups' language. This feature exemplifies not only the interruptive nature of gumboot dance, which allows for a shared language, a space for communication between those who have been structurally and consistently oppressed; this interruption also contains the communicative element of this form of dance. In these two moments there is a clear question-and-answer structure. The tension between contraction and release is choreographed into the dance. The soloist starts a new rhythm; the group replies. The body not only interrupts other means of signification which oppress it; it creates its own unique method of conversation, organised very much around discursive structures. This is a sequence of embodied grammar in motion.

That question-and-answer structure is a method of including more dancers; it creates an open structure for the choreography, enabling more dancers to participate, always opening the limits of possible interlocutors. The moving body invites more bodies to release into its motion. Within the context of body music more broadly this is a vital choreographic feature, allowing for the creation of an embodied space with permeable boundaries, inviting more dancers and recipients to join. The choreographic use of question-and-answer creates a chorus that is ever-expanding, going beyond its initial spatial grounding.

I read gumboot dance as an instance of sic-sensuous. It is an intervention and subversion in and of itself; it is a language that allows people to speak when they could not otherwise communicate. Gestures and movements are developed from a mining vocabulary into a highly elaborate and intricate aesthetic system of inscription. Gumboot dance creates a world and the language in which that world is communicated. Through dance, gumboot dancers are equal to those bodies that render them unequal, as they are utilising a different kind of language when they are banned from using verbal communication. They are saying 'no!' to the structures of oppression that deem them unequal by utilising their sensuous bodies.

Gumboot dancers become speaking beings when they are not allowed to speak. Gumboot dancers represent their lives in motion and in so doing subvert the systems that do not allow them to do so. As argued above, the use of clapping and stomping, as well as the question-and-answer structure, enables gumboot dancers to invite more and more dancers into the dance; more and more spectators to participate; more and more people to participate in radical moments of transgression by creating a shared embodied space. The dance elaborates and expands the tension between contraction into a single body and an ever-growing public sphere in motion.

Moving bodies writing on other moving bodies, and shifting their motion and rhythm, demanding constant attentiveness, create a shared embodied space. In this space they express their equality to each other as well as their individuality. Moreover, they express the equality to those who deem them unequal. Gumboot dancers develop a language where they are not able to do so otherwise. I proceed to release further into another instance of sic-sensuous, a clash between the strong reading of political dance, the subversive power of gumboot dance, and its use within *The Hungry Earth*, a play written in apartheid South Africa.

'Wake up, Mother Africa, Wake up, before the white man rapes you': gumboot dance and *The Hungry Earth*

Gumboot dance had an interesting collision with a verbal discussion of politics through its use in a play called the *The Hungry Earth*, written by Maishe Maponya in 1979. Maponya discusses the history of writing the play in the preface to his anthology; after conceiving the idea of the play in 1978, and doing a few performances with the Bahumutsi Drama Group at the Moravian Church Hall in Diepkloof, Maponya writes:

> I was struck by a sudden sense of insecurity. The play astounded audiences who had not seen such heavily political work before and their response prompted me to send a script for legal advice. I sent it to the lawyer via Bishop Desmond Tutu, then Secretary General of the SACC. In his reply to Bishop Tutu, attorney Raymond Tucker advised as follows: 'I am of the view that the play would constitute a contravention of the laws relating to racial incitement and the Publications Act and, in addition, the presentation would result in severe harassment of both the author and the performers' (Tucker R, 28 February 1978). (Maponya 1995: vii)

The play's performance was intertwined in the complex political structure of its time even before it was premiered. Later, Maponya decided to perform the play and be be 'damned' (Maponya 1995). Ian Steadman, who directed the play, writes that 'art can never be reduced to ideology or to sociological manifestation' (Steadman 1995: 5). He proceeds to argue against the title 'political play', as 'that label has connotations of a specific genre of theatre with didactic intentions ... the relationship between politics and performance in South Africa can perhaps best be summed up by saying that the subject matter is usually so steeped in politics that politics does not require a mention' (Steadman 1995: 5–6). There need be no explicit political reference in a play for it to be political; its structures of performance and reception are political in and of themselves. This play acted in the aesthetic register that I have been calling the strong reading of political dance.

The Hungry Earth is written in six scenes, including a choral epilogue. The first scene shows four black workers in a hostel room, sharing their stories of humiliation by white people. The second scene shows a sugar plantation with dire working conditions and child labour. The third scene depicts a train journey and shows police brutality towards the black workers. The fourth scene shows the mine, and both the working and the living conditions of miners. The last scene displays the death of a young miner and the subsequent lamentation by his wife. The function of language is crucial in the play: it uses Zulu at a time when Dutch, English and Afrikaans were the three official languages in South Africa (Gilbert 2001). Language symbolises hierarchy and segregation. Dance operates in the same register as Zulu within the play, noting inequality but also subverting it in its very performance, allowing those deemed unequal to speak.

The Hungry Earth was performed in South Africa in 1979 and then toured Europe in 1981. Both productions were directed by historian Ian Steadman (Fuchs 2002). Loots argues that *The Hungry Earth* is considered a landmark play in the context of South African protest theatre: 'It is an evocative powerful protest which uses theatre to demystify political and economic relations by focusing on short, sharp scenes of black working class life' (Loots 1997: 146). She shows the contradictions within the context of the writing and the performance of the play: whereas the play constructs the black male worker as a powerless victim, the actual performance of the play within and outside of South Africa did give voice to black working-class concerns. At the same time Loots notes that there is no voice for any differences within the black male working-class voice, and notably there is no space for women within the play; the only female black voice is given to a male actor. Fuchs reads the play as didactic, highlighting a song within the play with the lyrics 'wake up, Mother Africa,

Wake up, before the white man rapes you' (Fuchs 2002). Gilbert notes that *The Hungry Earth* was criticised for its portrayal of an idyllic and harmonious pre-colonial society, as well as for simplifying black–white relationships (Gilbert 2001). It is clear that, whether critiqued or endorsed, this play was important in South African theatre history as well as in the history of racial and economic inequalities within the country.

Gumboot dance has a crucial role in the play when it appears in scene 4. The dance is depicted as part of the exposition of miners' lives. On the role of the gumboot dance in the play Steadman notes: 'the gumboot dance in *The Hungry Earth*, the labour scenes in Imbumba, and he mining scene in Egolim cannot adequately be conveyed through textual means, but as theatrical performance they communicate dynamically about contemporary realities' (Steadman 1995: 2). Theatre scholar Helen Gilbert notes that 'the dance in scene Four can be read as a powerful act of resistance … yet this interpretation is turned on its head when the miners are subsequently asked to perform the dance for tourists on a Sunday' (Gilbert 2001: 14). Thus the reader–spectator can observe how the play utilises the dance as a theatrical device creating a moment of subversion within the text. The written play in itself was a subversion of the legal system, as discussed above. At the same time we see the complexity of the political implications of the dance, beyond a single-faceted reading of dance as resistance. The repetition of the dance shows the oppressive systems that created it in the first place. The play contracts from the use of verbal language into non-verbal expression in dance. But when the dance is released into repeated performance it exposes the structures of domination and oppression that underpinned the creation of gumboot dance within the everyday life of the miners.

Let us pause to consider the structural use of gumboot dance within this play; I see it as a clash between the weak reading of political dance and the strong reading. Ian Steadman supports this reading in his claim about the actual politics underlying the play and its performance: it need not articulate a verbal political message to be political; it is subversive in its articulation of the voice of the voiceless. At the same time, even within this reading dance occupies a unique position. It shows embodied resistance to the dire working conditions in which the miners worked and, simultaneously, how this moment of resistance and communication was appropriated by the hegemonic structures of symbolic power. The politics of dance here treads the boundary between resistance and appropriation; subversion and affirmation. The dance functions to communicate the reality of the leading characters in a way that cannot be narrated in words. The moment of dance within the play is thus dually interruptive. First, within the structure of the play itself, it is a moment of non-verbal communication within the verbal discourse. Second, gumboot dance within *The Hungry Earth* functions as the performance of subversion; it shows the miners' resistance to their marginalisation, to their being made others by not having access to language, thus not being able to interrupt through it.

Reading the play as rupture, the dance sequence within it is the zenith of that rupture. At the same time, the dance shows the structures of inequality within which the narrative of the play unfolds. The dancers perform the dance until they are exhausted after the long working day, as they are ordered to do so by those who deem them unequal. Initially the dance was used to break away from conditions which deprived the miners of a voice. They thereby created a world with its own shared space and embodied language. At the same time, when forced to be repeated by their superiors, the dance became a mechanism of disciplining; it enabled the white bosses to affirm their voice as superior. Dance can be, and has been, taken away from its subversive potential to sustain structures of power against which it arose. When taken away from the space that generated the gumboot dance – African miners – and utilised within a different embodied space – that of performance in front of the dancers' oppressors – any interruptive power originally held by the dance is lost.

I read this performance of gumboot dance as a further instance of sic-sensuous. The vocabulary of gumboot dance – taking mining actions and developing them into a choreographic vocabulary – has been read as one register of sic-sensuous, of the reinterpretation of movement as subversion experienced between two sensuous bodies. Performance of this vocabulary in conditions the miners do not choose for themselves results in further intervention, the use of that subversive power against equality. The white body forcing the black body to repeat its subversive dance interrupts its subversive power and reinforces the structures of inequality and domination that gave rise to it in the first place. This all occurs, once again, between two sensuous bodies without requiring verbal language. Moreover, when read in the context of the threatened action against the performance of the play, it leads to yet another contradiction; whereas the play in itself was subversive, the performance of gumboot dance (in the repeated version) actually reaffirmed the structures of domination the play interrupted.

Examining dance in the context of performance as well in the context of reception is vital when discussing its political power; releasing from one instance of performance into another may dramatically change the normative and conceptual power of dance as a political force.

Conclusions: a dance of their own

Gumboot dancers, in an ever-expanding line, or chorus, are crucial for the argument of this book. Releasing the unique vocabulary developed in South African gold mines by black miners into the context of apartheid in South Africa, while contracting into the unique setting that yielded this vocabulary of movement, shows the complexity of political dance. Gumboot dance is a political language that allows for the subversion of unequal structures grounded in racial and economic stratification. As a language, it includes both emancipatory and oppressive characteristics within it. As the reader–spectator has seen, those who have been deemed voiceless developed gumboot dance and thus they subverted the systems of signification that posited them as unequal. Gumboot dancers' use of dance as inscription, as a language of movement, was the subversive element of this intervention; their codification and their ability to utilise movement as a method of communication transgressed systems that deemed them unequal. They utilised that language to play the boundary between unison and solo, between individual and collective voice. At the same time, as seen in *The Hungry Earth*, the voice and system of inscription has been utilised by those who have marginalised the miners or dancers to consolidate the power systems that sustain racial and economic inequality.

Gumboot dance has subversive power when it is used by miners when they are not allowed to speak. It is used as a mechanism of oppression and reproduces conditions of inequality when those who create an intervention become merely entertainment for those whose systems of oppression they subverted. Thus we see here the distinct interplay between inscription read as an embodied language, a voice that becomes registered on moving bodies contracting into themselves and releasing into other bodies; and a different reading of inscription: as forced repetition which silences the embodied voice of the dancer. Revisiting the conceptual framework discussed in the first chapter, we see that the moment of interruption inscribes upon the bodies of the audience and dancers alike. However, that method of inscription, when imposed from above, reconsolidates the disciplining system within which the intervention occurred.

I conclude by releasing into a further register: the intersection between overt and covert politics of dance within the play; the clash between the weak and strong reading of political dance. In the choreographic language of the dance there is both subversion and affirmation; both individuality and suppression of a unique voice. The choreographic structures are open-ended, always inviting more people to participate as spectators or dancers. It is the use of dance as a language here that subverts the systems that deem some members of society as voiceless. At the same time, gumboot dance uses choreographic features which represent the oppressive conditions in which it was created. In its interplay between solos and unison the dance allows singular voices to intervene and fissure the seemingly cohesive choreography. Thus when we examine the language of gumboot dance we see that it is both subversive and disciplining. When we examine the reception of gumboot dance we see that it expands the community of sense to which it speaks. However, in some contexts, as in *The Hungry Earth*, the repetition of the dance and the privileging of the spectator over the dancer reproduces the systems of inequality which the dance subverted. Hence we see the clash between the weak and strong readings of political dance and proceed to read gumboot dance as operating on two registers. Gumboot dance is not all disciplining and is not all subversive on either reading. From the discussion of gumboot dance and its use within *The Hungry Earth* we learn about the complexity of dance as a political language. Dance was used here as a resource for those people who were not allowed to speak. When white spectators enforce repetition upon African miners they reinforce the structures of inequality from which those dancers dissented. Any reading of dance as a political language must be attentive to the interplay between subversion and appropriation as well as the conditions of reception in which the dance is performed.

I invite Johnny Hedebe, the gumboot dancer quoted at the beginning of this chapter, to close the argument which shows how gumboot dancers spoke for themselves. It is very clear that the miners developed a dance of their own. The gumboot dancers who have written their unique method of expression upon the space of my argument relentlessly ask the reader–spectator to be more attentive to the injustices and inequalities that structure our political world. South Africa went on to create one of the most progressive and egalitarian constitutions in the world, providing an example to many other countries lagging behind on issues of equality. Racial and economic inequalities are still constitutive to our world; the line of bent-over dancers, assigned to an inhumane space that endangered them daily, has expanded to other spaces of abuse and exploitation. Those lines of dancers are lines of individuals with a unique embodied voice, inscribing their equality upon those who marginalise them. Contracting within the body and placing it in an assigned space yields subversive and interruptive power. The expanding line of gumboot dancers invites the next set of dancers to enter the argument and protest against another form of structural inequality; the One Billion Rising movement protesting against gendered violence.

Note

1   All subheadings in this chapter are taken from Peter Abrahams's novel *Mine Boy*, apart from the final subheading, taken directly from Maishe Maponya's *The Hungry Earth*.

2   My emphasis.

5

Dancing the ruptured body: One Billion Rising, dance and gendered violence

I move the reader–spectator to view the performance of a protest movement that calls on us to end violence against women through the power of dance. One Billion Rising, initiated by feminist author and activist Eve Ensler, calls for a global uprising on Valentine's Day, utilising dance to protest against gendered violence. The impact of the movement has been far-reaching and its scope ambitious. The site of the movement is the moving body upon which gendered violence is inscribed and through which political interventions are brought into being. This chapter focuses on the connection between utilising the body as a mechanism of political intervention in the public space and interventions into the body itself.

One Billion Rising is a protest movement that explicitly utilises dance to convey a political message. I move from examining the movement's own interpretation of dance as it is communicated in words, the weak reading of political dance, to exploring the grassroots response to the movement's verbal message, and finally I discuss the reception of the movement's message, a moment of sic-sensuous. The chapter starts from a movement that tries to explicitly intervene in public spaces and positions women's bodies in protest against the degradation of women and girls around the world. The chapter ends in the individual resisting body that may not take on board One Billion Rising's message *tout court*. Nevertheless, the fractured body will respond to the call to oppose the marginalisation of female embodiment in its own way. Thus the chapter examines the reoccupation of space through dance on a dual level: both public spaces reinhabited by the moving body and the singular bodies composing this process and intervening in public spaces. The ruptured body contracts into itself and releases into a new public sphere, in which it is treated with dignity and respect, regardless of the intention of the founder of this movement.

One Billion Rising: dance against violence in ethos and practice

I invite the founder of One Billion Rising, Eve Ensler, to take centre stage. She discusses the ethos for the movement in her 2013 memoir, *In the Body of the World: A Memoir of Cancer and Connection.* The book recalls Ensler's struggle with liver cancer, explores her experience of being sexually molested by her father and her attempts to build the City of Joy, a healing space for women survivors of sexual violence in the Democratic Republic of the Congo (Ensler 2013a).[1] The memoir presents two parallel and interlinked narratives: Ensler's search for a healing space for herself following her detachment from her body throughout her life; and her engagement with structural violence against women in the Democratic Republic of the Congo. Thus the book tells of two structural/spatial interventions: Ensler's own journey to reinhabit her body as a space, contracting into the space of her body and reaffirming its spatiality; and her attempt to intervene in the global political space for other fractured bodies to heal themselves, releasing her personal journey towards other bodies. There has been ample feminist writing about the connection between gender, embodiment, violence and public spaces. In this chapter I focus on Ensler's unique reading and its influence on the One Billion Rising movement. Many other scholars have considered the relationship between space and the female body: one perspective focuses on physicality, materiality and the psyche (Gormley et al. 2008); another considers the relationship between the concept of the public sphere and the female body (Fraser 1990); further analysis problematises the relationship between everyday spaces and the female body (Rose 1999); and one specific angle examines sexual violence, space and the female body (Pain 1991). However, here I draw on Ensler's analysis only, with a focus on dance as a mechanism for intervention in space.

Dance plays a central role in the book's discussion of those parallel and interlinked processes. Ensler writes: 'Love isn't something else, something rising and surprising. It isn't aware of itself. It isn't keeping track. It isn't something you sign for. It's endless and generous and enveloping. It's in the drums, in the voices, in the bodies of the wounded made suddenly whole, by the music, by each other, dancing' (Ensler 2013a: 169). Dance for Ensler is a singular process through which the body can be made whole; dance aids through surprising tensions and contradictions.

She adds: 'when the women builders of City of Joy see me, they dance in the rain and mud. I dance with them. City of Joy is not finished' (Ensler 2013a: 196). It is clear that dance has a singular emotional and normative content for Ensler; although the City of Joy is not finished, the dance carries joy within it.

Elsewhere in the book, in a section called 'Leaking', she writes:

> I go to visit Esther, Mama of the wounded at Panzi Hospital. We do our ritual together with hundreds of the women survivors. We breathe, scream, kick, punch, release, and then there is mad drumming and we dance. I am still weak from the takedown and chemo, but it doesn't stop me. As I dance, I have no control over my bowels, and for the first time I don't care. Before when I was with the women and they were leaking from their fistulas, I could only imagine what it felt like. Now we are one wild mass of drumming, kicking, raging, leaking women. (Ensler 2013a: 198)

In this quotation Ensler is describing and analysing a moment of sharing through dance. In that moment she sees the unravelling of sensuous bodies towards each other. This is for Ensler a moment of abandonment, of release, which she aspires to push further. Dance enables Ensler to reoccupy her own body, experience love and a shared space with others, and she aims to unravel that in others. Her contraction into her own body is inextricably linked to release into other sensuous bodies. There is an irresolvable tension in this quotation between Ensler's own admission that she can only imagine what the women in the Congo feel like and the stark conceptual shift to a description of a wild mass of raging women. Dance connects different positions that are inhabited by different wounded bodies. Ensler here conflates equality and sameness: the ability of one moving body to respond to another with the knowledge of the sensation created by this shared space.

The feeling generated for Ensler through dance provides her with an interpretation of political dance as constituting a shared embodied space. The experience of dance enables her to appropriate her body as a world while revisiting all those forces which have inscribed upon her, all those networks of power that have written on her body and made it a world estranged to her. Ensler asks: can this feeling of the unravelling body, releasing to others, be used as a political platform to resist the violence which has wounded the body? Can the abandonment she feels within her own body be shared with other survivors of sexual violence? Can the process of contraction and release she has interpreted in words – through her own body – be transmitted to other bodies, wounded, hurting and inscribed by manifold languages of power, to be translated into a language of joy and dance? Can Ensler recreate this instance of release for others?

One Billion Rising's explicit reading of dance is intimately interlinked to the process described in Ensler's book. The movement's goal is stated online:

> One Billion Rising is the biggest mass action to end violence against women in human history. The campaign, launched on Valentine's Day 2012, began as a call to action based on the staggering statistic that 1 in 3 women on the planet will be beaten or raped during her lifetime. With the world population at 7 billion, this adds up to more than ONE BILLION WOMEN AND GIRLS. On 14 February 2013, people across the world came together to express their outrage, strike, dance, and RISE in defiance of the injustices women suffer, demanding an end at last to violence against women. Last year, on 14 February 2014, One Billion Rising for Justice focused on the issue of justice for all survivors of gender violence, and highlighted the impunity that lives at the intersection of poverty, racism, war, the plunder of the environment, capitalism, imperialism, and patriarchy. Events took place in 200 countries, where women, men, and youth came together to Rise, Release, and Dance outside of court houses, police stations, government offices, school administration buildings, work places, sites of environmental injustice, military courts, embassies, places of worship, homes, or simply public gathering places where women deserve to feel safe but too often do not (OBR 2013).

One in three women in the world will be beaten or raped during her lifetime. There are one billion potential victims of gendered violence. The movement calls upon those one billion potential victims to occupy public spaces considered loci of power. Thus the movement aims to show this statistic in moving bodies. The process through which Ensler occupied her own body as a world is narrated as a universal goal of re-appropriation public spaces for ruptured bodies everywhere. That re-appropriation takes place within the singular body and the public space in and through dance.

The movement provides a statement of its perception of dance, embodiment and resistance:

> Through trauma, cruelty, shame, oppression, violence, rape, exclusion, the body of the human species has been hurt, wounded, and we have been forced to flee our bodies.
>
> Dancing allows us to come back into our bodies as individuals and groups and a world, it connects our feet to the earth and inspires us to move to her rhythms. It allows us to go further, to include everyone, to tap into a revolutionary and poetic energy which is inviting us to take the lid off the patriarchal container, releasing more of our wisdom, our self-love. Our sexuality,

our compassion, and fierceness. Dancing is defiance. It is joyous and raging. It is contagious and free and beyond corporate or state control. We have only begun to dance. This year we must go further. We must go all the way and make the change. (OBR 2013)

This is a very specific reading of dance. Through this statement dance is assumed to be a power in and of itself, able to transform the body by creating a connection between the body and the earth. This connection is assumed to be already there and dance is assumed to bring the dancer back to a world hidden by injustice. The words 'contagious, free, beyond control, joyous', all used in this statement to describe dance, assume that the dance will release from one moving body to another. This reading of dance assumes that the unhinged, rebellious spirit will spread from one dancer to a seeming spectator who is ready to be galvanised, as we all are, in this struggle together, universally, and bring humanity back to a space beyond violence, suffering and oppression. The reading of dance here moves it away from its conceptualisation as a disciplined, inscribed language; it is unruly and disruptive. *Dance is interruptive in and of itself.* It is without contradictions. Dance hence can overcome state control and challenge the sovereign state in one of the most burning issues of our day: the widespread violence towards women and girls.

This interpretation argues that dance is a power independent of words. Moreover, dance can challenge other political systems and will engage increasing circles of people beyond the dancers themselves. Dance read through the One Billion Rising statement, and throughout this book, is able to transform the dancing bodies. Dance allows those dancing bodies to undergo processes otherwise inhibited by systems of power. The body is to be transformed and tap into resources it cannot reach under other systems of power. Dance is a political power in and of itself and can operate universally. Or can it?

Thus the One Billion Rising movement calls for a twofold spatial transformation: it calls for a transformation of the body as a space which has been invaded, taken away from its owners by structural violence that makes one billion women feel estranged from their own bodies; it calls for the reoccupation of the body as a space. Simultaneously the One Billion Rising movement calls for a transformation of the public spaces from which bodies of survivors of sexual violence are so often excluded. By so doing, the movement aims to shed light on the double trauma experienced by women survivors of violence who lose their body as a world and, at the same time, are not offered public spaces in which to recuperate and start a dialogue with other harmed female bodies, due to the fact that public spaces are always already masculine. Thus systems of power marginalise the female body and at the same time exclude it from spaces for healing. The One Billion Rising movement aims to undo this double marginalisation through dance. Releasing from a singular body, reoccupying it, allows it to reoccupy external spaces; contracting into the singular space of the ruptured body is intimately related to releasing into the shared world and, by so doing, changing its power structures.

Both Ensler's statements and One Billon Rising's official reading of dance and politics yield a reading of dance that may go even beyond the strong reading of political dance. Whereas the strong reading of political dance assumes that dance has a communicative power independent of other symbolic systems, it does not assume that power necessarily changes other political structures in the world. Indeed, this strong reading of political dance pauses on moments in which transgression occurs and inequalities and injustices in other symbolic systems become unravelled. Ensler and her followers assume an even stronger connection: they assume a direct causal link between reoccupying the body as a space through contracting into its systems of inscription and their reinterpretation, reoccupying public space in those re-inscribed bodies and changing perceptions and policies regarding violence against women and girls. The causality here is direct and strong, and assumes a one-directional change. That change moves from the moving ruptured body, to the healing space, to the change of state, court, NGO policy. That change is singular and cohesive. That change also implies an interpretation of dance as a singular and cohesive force.

At the same time, Ensler does inscribe a certain emotional and normative power within her interpretation of dance that moves towards the weak reading of political dance. Dance for her is joyful and emancipating; hence she takes it to be necessarily joyful and emancipating for other bodies partaking in the public space she is aiming to occupy. Ensler assumes her reinterpretation of inscription from violence to dance can be transferred to other bodies *tout court*. Thus we see a contradiction between the strong reading of political dance, the use of the newly constructed public sphere that One Billion Rising is creating in movement, and Ensler's definition of dance in words.

I invite those dancers who responded to Ensler's call to rise, strike, dance to take centre stage and inscribe upon the argument as it has thus far unfolded. From Duncan's dissent from ballet, through gumboot dancers forced to perform their embodied intervention for the enjoyment of those who marginalise them, dance has a dark side to it. Reading dance as a world, as Ensler and I attempt to do, requires a complex interpretation of dance as well as sensitivity to the conditions of its performance. When released from Ensler's body to others, the call generated by the One Billion Rising movement to rise, strike, dance around the world generated different responses which show the complexity of the world of dance for its various interlocutors. I invite the reader–spectator to listen to them now.

The flash mob as the non-universal

Eve Ensler writes about 'Break the Chain', the current anthem of OBR:

> Dance is dangerous, joyous, sexual, holy, disruptive, contagious, it breaks the rules. It can happen anywhere, anytime, with anyone and everyone, and it's free. Dancing insists we take up space, we go there together in community. Dance joins us and pushes us to go further and that is why it's at the center of ONE BILLION RISING. With infectious music and lyrics from Tena Clark, amazing vocals by a talented group of V-Girls, and Debbie Allen's bold choreography, Break the Chain is the anthem that will call up one billion to rise. (Ensler 2013b)

This statement reiterates the narrative that Ensler discusses in her book. It reads dance as abandonment, a force that spills from one moving body into a community of bodies responding to it. 'Break the Chain', the anthem for the One Billion Rising movement, is an American song performed by Tena Clark. Its lyrics are sung in English. The song is accompanied by an instructional video featuring Debbie Allen teaching the choreography which is supposed to be performed in the flash mob. (Allen was the ubiquitous dance teacher Lydia Grant in the 1980s television series *Fame*.) This is an intervention that provides its own choreographic language from above, from the embodied voice of the organiser of the movement. I will not discuss the set choreography here. Instead, I am interested in thirty-two counts at the beginning of the routine which are defined in the instructional video as 'improvisation' and the divergences within it in various performances of the flash mob. These counts are the only parts of the song that don't have lyrics in English.

In San Francisco (www.youtube.com/watch?v=WufjSyE_rK8) this sequence is highly choreographed and ordered; it starts with women crawling between women carrying info-like signs commenting on statistics related to the prevalence of sexual violence. They are later picked up by women, and join together in uniform movement. Clearly, all the women know their position in space and their role in the group ahead of the flash mob. A sharp distinction exists between the moments of anticipation before the dance commences and the beginning of the dance sequence, which is organised on the theme of connecting the women and creating a non-verbal dialogue, first starting in movement mimicking despair, then reaching out to another woman, being lifted, then joining the mass movement in the improvisation part of the song. In the following parts of the song the dancing bodies contract into their own embodied space. In looking at individual movers within this sequence, all moving in a similar movement, reaching out, opening up towards the sky, each one becomes entrenched within her own embodiment, opening up, releasing within her own space. The only part of the video in which we see engagement between the dancers is the highly choreographed opening sequence. At the same time, the unison effect of the movement means that the women create a space through that movement; their delving deeper into themselves creates an external boundary, a mass pointing towards the sky, opening up as if they are one body.

This highly choreographed and disciplined start of the flash mob differs markedly from the beginning of the flash mob in the Congo (www.youtube.com/watch?v=u4YJZ2NB4Vk). The movement does not seem to ve co-ordinated. The dancers rarely engage with each other or the camera; it is clear they are immersing themselves in the movement, contracting into their own bodies. This clip is also vastly different to the San Francisco flash mob in the fact that a number of performers are men. Is this a movement for solidarity between men and women or the colonialisation of a female space by men? This video does not provide with answers. The women do not engage with the men's presence. At the same time, let us not make assumptions about these women's experience and leave this question open. Once again the key movements are those of opening the chest and arms to the sky, re-appropriating space by demarcating ever-growing circles around the dancers. The upper body is released into the space around it.

In Tamera, Portugal (www.youtube.com/watch?v=kMgodbupkcI), we again see a choreographed beginning but it is different from the San Francisco clip. As in the Congo we see a large group of men within the dancers. The dancers start moving in a small group, reaching out to the sky. They start by kneeling and pointing towards the sky, slowly spreading and taking up more space. The dancers in this clip seem much more sombre than in the two other clips discussed. The movement is less referential than the motion seen in the Francisco flash mob. The notable feature of this take on the open-ended beginning is the visible spreading of the dancers to occupy space by movement. The dancers are engrossed in the movement itself, contracting into each individual body. From a densely organised group they spread out and inhabit more physical space. This is a choreographic response to the call to occupy public space by moving bodies. The use of release to acquire more space for the body is a central characteristic of the choreography.

In Sudan (www.youtube.com/watch?v=Panv2wVSvGI – the clip discussed appears in the video from 11:30 onwards) there is an unchoreographed response to the beginning of the dance sequence. The dancers seem immersed in their own world. In this sequence the focus is specifically on the dancers' arms. As in the Portuguese version they point towards the sky; however, they also point towards other dancers. This seems to be a spontaneous movement rather than an organised one as we see very little co-ordination between the various dancers. The dancers in this clip are static in their space; their arms become the boundaries of their bodies, extending outward and inward, encircling in and out, painting an invisible boundary that keeps expanding. The extent of release here is quite limited within the spatiality of each body rather than releasing into a wider space as the accumulation of all bodies.

In a version performed by the New Light Girls in India (www.youtube.com/watch?v=KYS3NinY4Cc) there is once again a co-ordinated beginning, which includes a similar motif to the improvised versions discussed above. Once again the movement utilises arms encircling and pointing outwards from the moving bodies. The dancers shift their weight from side to side, while the crux of the movement consists in encircling the arms through space, moving to continuously occupy a space that is bigger than their own bodies. Once again we see an opening of the torso towards the sky. Release here does not move a singular body beyond a static position in space; the boundaries between the different bodies do not seem porous.

In the Wiesbaden version (www.youtube.com/watch?v=lYx_Y9i673k) we see another way of occupying more space with minimal movement: the dancers shift their weight from side to side, thus creating again the image of a circle, ever enlarging itself, ever expanding in space. For those who would claim that the ability to utilise the body to take more space depends on virtuosity, this video proves otherwise; by mere shifting of weight *en masse* we are given a powerful image of the extension of the body out of itself. Release comes in various methods and systems of inscription and does not determine a particular choreographic vocabulary. It does not even require movement of the limbs beyond shifting the weight from one foot to the other. Bodies can expand in space and towards each other in manifold, subtle ways.

I pause here to note that, that with the exception of the first version discussed – the stylised San Francisco flash mob, in which a dialogue between the dancers was highly choreographed and integrated into the performance – none of the dances show much engagement of the dancers with each other; indeed, in many of the versions few of them actually acknowledge the camera or whoever is behind it. Sometimes, as in the start of the Indian version, the camera captures a fleeting smile, but in many of the versions we see that the call to improvise and explore the movement results in a self-enclosed response, exploring the body's corporeality, density, inscription within itself rather than the joyful carnivalesque abandonment that Ensler preaches. The reception of Eve Ensler's message has created a universal sphere of sic-sensuous, of multiple interpretations that do not follow her call but are politically powerful, both for the bodies they inhabit and for the public sphere they create within the context of their performance.

Then there are the One Billion Rising videos that do not use the song, or the choreography, of 'Break the Chain' at all. In Panay, the Red Detachment of Women NPA Panay perform to a local song, with aerobic-like exercises in military outfits (www.youtube.com/watch?v=Gey1CWznaPg). I now move to focus on this performance as an example of what I have been discussing throughout the book as sic-sensuous; of the transmission of meaning, of dialogue between bodies that does not necessitate words and transgresses politics as articulated in words. While it would seem unlikely that a military unit of the Communist Party engages in a flash mob, this is their own embodied response to the call to rise, strike, dance that the One Billion Rising movement generated. In this clip too we see dancers pointing their fingers towards the sky, encircling space around the women's bodies. The dancers' faces are hidden, they are serious and coordinated. There is nothing joyful about this version; it looks no different from military drills. The sequence ends with the women firing their guns towards the sky. There could not be a more different response to Ensler's depiction of dance as 'dangerous, joyous, sexual, holy, disruptive, contagious, it breaks the rules'. This clip shows an intervention into Ensler's message in the language of dance itself. It shows perhaps the strongest sic-sensuous of all performed versions; its language of movement stands in sharp opposition to Ensler's narration of dance in words. And yet, for its performers, this dance creates an opportunity for sensed bodies to come together and reoccupy their own space.

The same music to the song danced in Panay, as well as an almost identical choreography (save for the arm pointing towards the sky at the beginning instead of pointing down), feature in a less military context, in Hong Kong (www.youtube.com/watch?v=JPhqtNFf2c8). In this version women wear the One Billion Rising T-shirts; they appear just as uniform as the women soldiers, but in their civilian uniform. Later, they move into 'Break the Chain', with the beginning highly choreographed and providing a literal response to the lyrics. Once again we see the tension between the dancers releasing into their environment and their delving into their own bodies.

In Batticola, India, women in saris drum uniformly on the beach (www.youtube.com/watch?v=l7cIq3ZXHRM). There is no music apart from the women's drums; slowly, the performers start shifting into a circle; they move their weight from side to side as in the Wiesbaden clip discussed above. The dancers turn around in their place; they begin to hop as they move around the circle; and then they return to minute weight-shifting from side to side, leaning in and out of the circle. Now the weight-shifting allows them to play with the boundaries of the circle. Next, they move their weight to the centre of the circle, and release their chests to the sky, opening up both their individual bodies and the entire circle as a spatial formation, simultaneously, to the space surrounding them. Now the rhythm is faster and the circle becomes self-enclosed; we notice the audience clapping, following the rhythm.

It is remarkable that, whether choreographed or not, co-ordinated or not, performed to the official anthem 'Break the Chain' or to different music, all the videos express several movement motifs that repeat themselves. First, as noted, there is the use of arms pointing towards the sky, sideways and outside of the body. The body questions its boundaries, expanding in space, moving beyond its initial demarcated place, and occupies a bigger space than the space it had occupied when the dance began. The moving body shows that it can take up a larger space than it takes up before moving. This choreographic feature becomes even more evident when we look at the accumulation of bodies, all moving together in this movement motif; we see a mass of people who shift the boundaries of their assigned space and enlarge it further. In the Tamil version discussed above we see a striking use of space, when women move from the centre of the circle towards its outer space, incorporating both motifs together. In this version the dancers use the motif of the circle, while drumming, to occupy a larger space than the one from which they started. There is a repeat of the use of arms and circles to enlarge the space the body takes in the world. When bodies move together they enlarge the space the group of women take in the world. We see manifold interpretations of the concept of release within the body and between two moving bodies.

These are various choreographic responses to what I have been reading throughout the book as release: motion shifting from one inscribed
body to others with which it is sharing space. Whereas Martha Graham
used one technical interpretation of release, we see that there are many
interpretations of this choreographic idea which do not necessitate dance
education. Dance gains power when it shifts from one moving body to
another.

At the same time, the continuity of the movement exemplified by the
use of circles out, but also in, explores the body as a space in and of itself.
The arms extend outward but also inward; the dancers' bodies assume
a different position within themselves. Circles mean not only expanding outward but also exploring the space of the body inward. The arms
become more and more outstretched with every circle; the body explores
not only its placement within space but also its density within itself.
Thus we must not only focus on the obvious, overt element repeating
itself here, the enlarging of the body in circles. We must shift our gaze
towards the implications this circular movement has for the corporeality of the dancers; the space of the body inwards. We see here manifold
bodies contracting into themselves, bringing into conflict configurations
of violence and power that have been written on multiple bodies globally
and their own unique danced response to those configurations of power.
Contraction here is just as political as the overt intention to release, if not
more so.

Finally, the most significant point arising from these various clips is
their lack of uniformity. There are numerous systems of inscription utilised by the dancers. Some of these systems of inscription seem more
in tune than others with the explicit message of the One Billion Rising
movement and its conception of dance as joyous rupture. Some methods of inscription seem highly disciplined and disciplining. Dance is
utilised to intervene in the public space; but at the same time it carries
within it many systems of signification that are far from being unruly.
The women performing military exercises in uniform and firing their
guns in the air present a completely different set of meanings to the that
presented by Ensler. Yet those women, as all other dancers in the clip,
respond to Ensler in the same language in which she created the One
Billion Rising movement: dance. We see here a powerful instance of sic-
sensuous: transgression articulated through dance between sensuous
bodies: Eve Ensler's body and the manifold bodies who responded to her
in diverse systems of inscription. I move to contract further into another
register of the argument.

Conclusions: the failure of universality and the transformation of the body: rising together beyond unison

This chapter started with Eve Ensler's experience of sharing an unruly moment with the women of the Congo through dance. Women and men all over the world had showed her that resistance to violence can be undergone in a variety of systems of inscription. Eve Ensler's body may have catalysed this movement but it certainly could not determine the responses generated from bodies assembling around the idea of the movement. The response to the discipline of the body is not unruly movement; rather, it is a contesting language, which expresses through and with the body ideas of resistance, anger and above all the fact that women's bodies deserve to take up much more space than that to which they are assigned. Moreover, they show that they do not have to be instructed on how to release into space; and they can share a moment of sensation while showing those characteristics which create differences between all those moving – and moved – bodies. The concept of sic-sensuous carries heavy political weight.

Some of the participants in the One Billion Rising flash mob in Baltimore reflected on the event. They wrote:

> By performing the same choreographed moves to the official 'One Billion Rising' theme song, Break the Chain, Hopkins students became part of the global movement to demand an end to GBV.[2] Historically, dance has been used a form of activism. However, only recently have people begun to see its power for global activism. Even today, some of the most conservative cultures in the world ban organized dance. It is feared, because it ignites the one thing that you cannot take away from a person: hope. (Branchinia et al. 2013: 252)

This short paragraph narrating some of the participants' experience in the flash mob highlights the contradictions I have discussed throughout the chapter. The One Billion Rising movement offers a specific point of view, namely Western, utilising a song in English to create what is meant to be a global platform for movement. Yet those who have taken up the call to rise, strike, dance have done so in manifold ways, performing in their own methods of inscription. The One Billion Rising dancers draw upon one interpretation of dance – as an unruly power which penetrates structures of domination in diverse languages. At the same time the responses to violence inscribed upon women's and girls' bodies – which are necessarily different and multifarious – are different and multifarious too. The Johns Hopkins participants cannot really share a global platform of uniform performances of dance as there is no such globalised cohesive interpretation. Revisiting the discussion of shared space in this book, including kinaesthetic empathy in Chapter 1 as well as the discussion of Martha Graham and the reception of her work in Chapter 3, I draw attention to a conceptual overlap. Once again a white body, this time Eve Ensler's, presents itself as universal and crates a space of shared sensation derived from its own experiences. At the same time, examining the danced responses shows there are manifold methods of resistance to this particularity presented as universalism. Ensler founded a space for sic-sensuous. Each one of the dancers, responding to the ethos of the One Billion Rising movement in their own system of inscription, exemplifies the resistance available within the moving body. The key lesson we learn is that the fact that dance can go beyond boundaries does not mean that is a universal language. Rather, I argue, the capacity to use dance as a subversive mechanism is universal. The body is not universal but the body is able to intervene universally.

Moreover, the clips we have discussed yield a far more complex and contradictory reading of dance than that presented by Ensler and appropriated by the One Billion Rising movement. Dance is unruly and disciplined, intervening and continuous. The top-down instructions created by the One Billion Rising movement provided the starting point for the transgression and subversion of its choreographed language. Every clip shows other moments in which the system of inscription is obliged by languages inscribed upon the dancers' bodies. Each response exemplifies the characteristics of the lived worlds of the dancers. The dancers have opened for the reader–spectator a vista into the dancers' unique life experience and the way they interpret resistance to gendered violence. Each moment of sic-sensuous unravelled a body that contracted into itself and released into a shared space. The failure to create a universal unison of resistance is the triumph of a more complex interpretation of dance, arising from an individual body but never disengaged from its unique lived experience. We are reminded here of Isadora Duncan's rebellious toes that refused to obey; multiple rebellious toes contested the universalism of One Billion Rising in their own unique ways.

And yet there are some choreographic characteristics present in all the clips discussed. In all of those danced instances moving bodies occupy space together. Those bodies create a danced relational presence in numerous public spaces around the world. They release from their own embodied space into a shared space, a non-verbal public sphere, inhabited by dancers seeking to affirm the need to treat bodies with respect. The response to the call to rise, strike, dance is made in the dancers' own embodied languages and always through dance. All these responses affirm the independence of dance as a world. Eve Ensler created a global message in which dancers dissented from violence against women. In so doing they also dissented from a top-down narrative of *how* this resistance should be narrated. Dancers around the world triumphed in the One Billion Rising mission of reoccupying their bodies through motion and at the same time occupying public spaces. They brought their own worlds into that global movement. The failure to create a unified choreographic interpretation of the weak reading of political dance as solely joyful and explosive results in multiple versions of the strong reading of political dance. Sic-sensuous results in manifold interpretations of the relationship between contraction into the ruptured body and release into a shared global space constituted around the message of ending violence against women and girls. This strong political reading cannot ever be conceptualised as a global language since it draws on numerous lived experiences of moving bodies. Those bodies intervene and bring their own systems of inscription to the moment of performance.

Whereas gumboot dancers who were assigned to a demarcated space subverted it by using physical mechanisms of protecting their bodies from injury in dire working conditions – their gumboots – One Billion Rising allows the body to contest its vulnerability in other ways. Through intervening in spaces within and without the injured body, and through creating embodied dialogue between multiple subjects who either underwent or are in danger of sexual violence, the power of the bodies of women comes to the forefront of the public sphere. Thus the dancers of One Billion Rising write a significant message upon the body of this argument. Those dancers, in their multitude of responses to Eve Ensler's call to rise, strike, dance, show that there is power within the female body to resist oppression and degradation. The lives of these women who rise may not coincide with each other; each faces a different set of challenges and threats; and yet they are all able to come together within their own local space. These women contest their vulnerability by showing the force of the body of women as opposed to the body of woman. The One Billion Rising dancers write on the body of this argument one of its most fundamental messages: the body is never purely vulnerable, neither to violence nor to cultural imperialism, even from the best intentions.

The One Billion Rising movement has managed to create a global platform against gendered violence, albeit sometimes contrary to its founding message in words. In the next chapter I push the reader–spectator to explore further the tension between the universal and the particular, the moving body and structures of violence, when I read the concept of human rights through dance. Thus the argument releases further from a shared sphere of activism and dissent into legal-political frameworks that constitute our global body politic.

Notes

1   The Congo has been defined by a Margot Wallstrom, the UN's special representative on sexual violence in conflict, as 'the rape capital of the world'. The UN Joint Human Rights Office in the DRC (UNJHRO) released an in-depth report which documents serious incidents of sexual violence in the country, with over 3,600 victims registered by the office between January 2010 and December 2013.

2   Gender-based violence.

6

Dancing human rights

We have seen that ever since Isadora Duncan entered the stage of political dance, various instances of sic-sensuous have been performed on the stage of the argument by bodies contracting into themselves and releasing to other bodies, moving and being moved. Those bodies affirm their equality to other bodies – whether the dancing bodies they intervene against, or bodies inhabiting other worlds that deem them unequal. From Martha Graham's audiences who are uninvited spectators to the gumboot dancers in South Africa and the flash mob dancers of One Billion Rising, manifold bodies keep performing their equality and dissent against voices which marginalise them. This concluding chapter contracts into the crux of legal and political theory from which the book arises. This book has shown how dance can intervene in legal and political structures that marginalise human beings. Consequently this chapter moves to argue that dance can protest injustice while always remaining grounded in the local setting from which it arose, and yet transcend it. The chapter consequently rearticulates the argument of the book within the context of the language and problematics of human rights. The chapter works through a dual argument. First, it argues that dance can be utilised to protest human rights violations. Second, the chapter presents a reading of human rights through sic-sensuous, an inscribed dialogue between two moving bodies creating aesthetic and political rupture. This conception sees subjects able to live in two worlds at the same time: one in which they cannot claim their human rights and one in which they affirm their ability to claim those rights. I argue that dance enables the conceptualisation of human rights in movement.

The reader–spectator is summoned to observe two instances of tension between contraction and release: within the world of dabke dancers in

Palestine and within the body of Arkadi Zaides, an Israeli choreographer who performs protest against human rights violations in his work Archive.

Human rights in a performed sic-sensuous

The theoretical backdrop against which I work in this chapter is the concept of the paradox of human rights. The interpretation of human rights as paradoxical, briefly defined, is derived from the recognition that human rights appeal to the universal, global or transcendent; they are said to belong to all people no matter who or where they are. On the other hand, humans realise their rights only in particular places with particular instruments and particular protections (Stern and Straus 2014). Specifically, this interpretation of human rights as paradoxical enable us to turn the spotlight upon those who are unable to claim human rights – those human beings for whom this discrepancy between global legitimacy and local mechanisms for rights claims is more than a jurisprudential and political conundrum but rather a challenging everyday reality. Hannah Arendt, who, in a celebrated and often-quoted paragraph, wrote about the right to rights, sheds light upon this paradox. Her reading of rights focused on the stateless, for whom local mechanisms of claiming human rights did not exist.

> The calamity of the rightless is not that they are deprived of life, liberty and the pursuit of happiness, or of equality before the law and freedom of opinion – formulas that were designed to solve problems within given communities – but that they no longer belong to any community whatsoever. Their plight is not that they are not equal before the law, but that no law exists for them; not only are they oppressed but that nobody even wants to oppress them. (Arendt 1976: 296)

Arendt's paragraph has been problematised and interpreted widely. Many theorists have reread it in the context of our present-day legal-political structures and their resulting problematics, or have been inspired by it to draw up their own analysis of human rights, for example Agamben (1998), Ariela Azoulay (2015), Etiene Balibar (2007), Seyla Benhabib, especially in her *Another Cosmopolitanism* (with responses from Jeremy Waldron, Bonnie Honig and Will Kymplicka) (2006), Ayten Gündoğdu (2015) and James D. Ingram, who specifically looks at connections between Arendt and Rancière (2008).

In 'Who is the Subject of the Rights of Man?' Rancière notes an example of the enactment of human rights in a space and time yet to be established; in a world yet to be built. Rancière uses as an example Olympe de Gouge, who as a woman was not an equal citizen, but who stated that if women were entitled to go to the scaffold they were also entitled to go to the Assembly (Rancière 2010). Women were equal 'as men' under the guillotine, thus de Gouge mobilised this equality in death to the whole of equality, including political equality. Rancière's example is an embodied one, juxtaposing the right to life and death under the guillotine in a particular human body; that argument allows us to move towards further moments of performing sic-sensuous in an embodied way, through dance.

Beyond the logical, jurisprudential and ontological gap between the universality of the legitimating mechanisms of human rights and the ability to claim them in particular settings resides the commitment to equality. If that commitment to equality is taken seriously it demands further investigation into mechanisms through which subjects can claim human rights despite the tension between the local and the universal. I proceed to release into a different discussion of the paradox of human rights through the concept of sic-sensuous; of two bodies inscribing upon each other and affirming both their equality and difference; bringing into clash two worlds: one in which they may be perceived as marginal and the world of the strong reading of political dance in which two sensuous bodies conversing always affirm their equality.

Dance scholars Naomi Jackson and Toni Shapiro-Phim, editors of a volume engaging dance, human rights and social justice, focus their analysis on the use of dance as a tool for revealing, resisting and rectifying differing forms of abuse and injustice (Shapiro-Phim 2008). They flesh out dance's power to bridge diverse communities as well as heal wounds of individual hurt bodies, two themes explored throughout this book. Reading dance as enabling bottom-up protests against human rights abuses as well as articulating equality where it is not yet recognised brings it into conversation with the theoretical limelight of the paradox of human rights as well as reading dance through the concept of sic-sensuous. I have highlighted throughout this book the concepts of dance as enduring beyond a single utterance (which I interpret as inscription) and dance as transformative for the dancing body and its relationship to its surroundings (which I read as sharing embodied space). The concept of sic-sensuous allows me to release the argument into a different theoretical space, demarcated by the literature of the paradox of human rights.

The term sic-sensuous has been understood throughout the book as carrying a threefold significance. First, as a refusal to follow the rules of the beautiful or aesthetically acceptable. Second, the term always implies writing on the body by another body. Third, the term looks at moments of slippage of meaning articulated by one moving body and received by a body that is moved. The term sic-sensuous allows for the performance of writing of one sensuous body upon another, and for the creation of a shared embodied space in that moment of writing. This shared embodied space is grounded between those two bodies that are able to converse without requiring words. At the same time, the moment of sharing illuminates the difference between those two bodies. The concept of sic-sensuous illuminates the grounding of the moving body in the communities in which it partakes and towards which it releases. This interaction between two moving bodies takes place in manifold acts of inscription. Those acts of writing shared between sensed bodies allow the subject to move beyond the boundaries of its own spatiality as well as to transcend the boundaries of communities in which it partakes. This argument gains further significance in instances in which some of those communities essentially marginalise dancing subjects and deem them unequal citizens of those communities.

Reading the concept of sic-sensuous in the context of the human rights paradox is significant for three reasons:

Firstly, shifting the limelight towards political spaces constructed by dance allows for the performance of equality of some subjects that may have been deemed unequal in politics articulated in words. The doctrine of human rights requires political and legal frameworks, allowing subjects to claim those rights as equals. Focusing on communities articulated in movement allows for the expansion of the performance of equality.

Secondly, the argument of this book, inspired by the ethos of the human rights doctrine, is grounded in the assumption that all human beings are created equal. They are, however, never perceived as the same. Articulated in moments of shared sensation between bodies that are equal but that may be interpreted as unequal in politics articulated in words, moments of sic-sensuous allow for the performance of differences between human bodies. Those differences, performed through dance, may illuminate the inequalities that may deem some bodies unequal. Thus this conceptual focus allows for the unravelling of instances of oppression and discrimination that stand in the way of full enforcement of the human rights doctrine. Those moments may go unnoticed when focusing on verbal language only.

Thirdly, sic-sensuous focuses on acts of inscription that go beyond one singular performance. When subjects are denied spaces to perform their equality they may create alternative spaces through dance. Those spaces are not momentary interventions. They are lasting spaces of resistance towards human rights abuses. This allows for further attentiveness of the reader–spectator towards acts of opposition against the degrading and deprivation of dignity.

I seek to find moments in which dance is utilised from the bottom up, protesting a wrong, namely the marginalisation of individuals who are deemed voiceless, less than human. I draw my case studies from one of the areas which is of key interest to human rights activists and theorists worldwide. This is the struggle of the Palestinian people for sovereignty and recognition as a state under international law. This struggle enables the people of Palestine to make human rights claims within jurisprudential structures that belong to a nation state. This struggle occurs against the backdrop of the Israeli occupation and consequent human rights abuse. The first subjects inscribing their human rights are dabke dancers, performing Palestine's national dance.

Dabke: political space for a sovereign state in the making

In a study of dabke on the West Bank, Mauro Van Aken notes that ritual practices and embodied identities have seldom been studied in Palestinian literature (Aken 2006). Nicholas Rowe, who in his book *Rising Dust* has conducted the most extensive study of dance in Palestine available to date, commences his discussion of dabke by noting that it is the most publicly promoted form of dance in the contemporary West Bank (Rowe 2010).[1] Rowe argues that dabke functioned to maintain solidarity and cohesion in the community. Van Aken notes that in haflas, celebratory evenings, dakbke can be learned by imitating others. He adds that musicians, dancers and the audience may swap roles. The dance is essentially participatory and encourages its spectators to become part of its shared space when it is performed. At the same time this characteristic is enabled by creating a shared embodied space which is constituted in a shared system of inscription. The dance constantly moves towards further spatial release.

The history of dabke in Palestine is a history of clashes between the weak and strong readings of political dance. Prior to 1967 dabke was a distinctly rural practice. After 1967 dabke crossed class divides. It became a pan-Palestinian dance expressing on the one hand the ongoing tensions with Israel and on the other hand relationships with other Arab countries in the region. The rallies of different political factions in the West Bank during the 1970s also became locations for the dancing of dabke. By the late 1970s, major political parties had dabke groups, and dabke featured as a centrepiece of political rallies. It was performed outside the realm of partisan politics; it was performed at nationalistic events designed to emphasise Palestinian identity through the Heritage Centre, and local folklore festivals featuring displays of dabke were held in public gardens throughout the 1970s. These were increasingly subject to censorship by the Israeli military. According to Rowe: 'dabke troupes were denied permission to travel between towns, and individuals attempting to promote dabke became subject to house arrest, detention, interrogation, imprisonment and physical abuse' (Rowe 2010: 119). The power of dabke as a national dance was noted beyond its Palestinian spectatorship. This power was threatening enough to elicit official state intervention from the entity that Palestine seeks emancipation from: the Israeli Occupation. Dabke creates a space in which the Palestinian people are sovereign over themselves, even in conditions in which they cannot be equal before international law. That space is performed independently of the discussion of dabke in spoken words, its affiliation with parties of performance in various political settings. At the same time, the shared space created by dabke does not go unnoticed by the regime, which consistently acts to deny the Palestinian people its sovereignty. The power of dabke is understood very well by the Israeli government, which seeks to tame it and control it. And yet the dance sustains. It is a space for resistance to consistent human rights abuses.

It should be noted that thus far, drawing on Rowe's analysis, the focus has been on the West Bank. In a study of dabke in the Jordan Valley, Mauro Van Aken argues that whereas dabke is perceived in the West Bank as a strong symbol of national identity, in the Jordan Valley it does not constitute an official discourse of dispossessed culture. Rather, he argues, performance of dabke allows for the constitution of a public space allowing for the revelation of relations of identity (Aken 2006). I draw on both readings together to argue that dabke allows for a space for contestation of identities and discourses. At the same time, those contestations and those differences are negotiated within a shared language, that of dabke. Dabke allows for the release of dancing bodies into a shared space when international law denies them that space. It also allows them a space to perform both their equality and their difference; those characteristics that bind them together and those characteristics that make them unique bodies.

The paramount dabke group performing on stage, El Fanoun, was interpreted as ideologically aligned with the socialist Popular Front for the Liberation of Palestine (PELP), but, in the words of one of its founders, started to distance itself from the political slogans of Palestinian factions and asked: 'are we doing dabke for art, or just for posters for a political party? It was not our idea to become a dancing group for any political party' (Rowe 2010: 136). I read in this statement the clash between the weak reading of political dance, or dance subsumed to political slogans, and the strong reading of political dance, defined here as 'dabke for art'. Let us contract into the dance itself and see dabke as art representing the Palestinian people within and outside their polity.

Rowe reads dabke as serving as 'a traumatic reminder of the imagined past, as its conscious revival was inextricably linked to the notion of a violent break with the past' (Rowe 2010: 117). Van Aken sees dabke as 'swinging between ideals of reproduction of past identity, assumed as a contemporary cultural symbol, and the local reinvention and exhibition of creativity and cultural challenge' (Aken 2006: 206). Further, the displaced cultural tradition of dabke is reinterpreted to become a new symbolic resource – 'an important medium both for defining belonging and difference and in the way of "making place" in displacement' (Aken 2006: 205). Thus dabke has operated as a public sphere in which ideas of identity and belonging have been negotiated within Palestine. It has enabled the sharing of an embodied space between sensed bodies that are not allowed that space elsewhere; they can, through dabke, mark their equality to each other and to their oppressors. I now contract further into one instance of dabke, performed informally, and bring one dabke group into the limelight of the argument.

The expanding line of the dabke dance into a state-in-becoming

(www.youtube.com/watch?v=bdrGrRmdvfA)

There are several choreographic characteristics the reader–spectator can note in this clip. First, the dance shifts in its levels of energy. It starts quietly, generates momentum, calms down and reinvigorates itself throughout. The switch between contraction and release occurs through the beat as well as through the movement. The dance is very rhythmical – there is stomping throughout the dance, and from its very beginning and throughout there is audience clapping in the background. The performers and spectators share responsibility in generating the underlying rhythm for the piece, and this is sustained throughout. The use of rhythm, as noted by Van Aken,

> is connected to a labour practice and to a specific rhythm of work; when the dancers/labourers had a leaking roof, the owner of the house would call his neighbours for help and the neighbours would gather on the roof. They would hold hands, form a line and start stamping their feet while walking on the roof in order to adjust the mud. (Aken 2006: 221 n. 5)

The sources of the rhythmic nature of the dance, then, are both referential and practical; they relate to a commonly shared experience from the past, but sustain physically that element of participatory openness, of a line that is meant to grow longer. Its use of body music is similar to that employed in gumboot dance, discussed in Chapter 4. In both these dances clapping and stomping allow more dancers to join the dance, and hence allow its shared space (and consequently its potential subversion as a space of resistance) to expand.

Spatially, the group performing the dance keeps its formation in space stable. Whether by holding hands or creating other references to each other, the dance moves from what appears to be one body. At the same time, there is one dancer, called the lawih, who holds a stick, who sometimes breaks from the group and rejoins it. There is a tension between this choreographic leadership role and the unison movement of the group. The shift between contraction and release hence occurs between the singular body and the group from which it emerges. This spatial characteristic allows the dancers to create a moving body larger than all their individual bodies combined; an entity larger than the separate individuals; a moving collective. Van Aken argues that the aspiration is for the group to create a common body. He writes: 'ideally, the group of dancers should become a common body. That body is interrupted by an increasingly faster rhythm used to emphasised a collective tempo' (Aken 2006: 209). The shifting collective is larger than the sum of its components; the one dancer breaking away and returning shows that very forcefully. This choreographic structure allows for spatial openness; people can join the line naturally without disturbing it and yet there are clear structures to follow. The dance, then, allows both for sharing and for interruption; for participating and for inserting another moving body into an already established formation. Here again we see the tension between equality and individuality; as Arendt had argued, it is the equality of the dancers that allows them to respond to each other; it is their individuality that pushes them to break away from the line.

Van Aken also notes that the dabke line is meant to move in a horizontal line but in practice often stands in a circular formation, led by the lawih (Aken 2006). This choreographic configuration, Van Aken notes, allows for shifts in energy to be organised; dancers can follow the leader and yet join at any point of the dance. He adds that the collective movement is characterised by continuous advancement and retreating, responding to changing rhythms. This is a clear instance of tension between contraction and release. Thus Van Aken reads dabke as a form of controlled tension towards collective dance, a collective body, a common feeling, in which the boundary between dancers and spectators remains constantly fluid. Dance is the method of demarcating space, through the dancing body that becomes inscribed by this dance and spectatorship.

The lawih, the group leader, according to Van Aken, should be able to co-ordinate, to put the dancers into play and let them to dance in a harmonious way; he should be able to generate intimacy and empathy, and at the same time to create order within the performance (Aken 2006). The leader of the group is the demarcating line, a living boundary who is able to draw participants into the dance and at the same time organise them and create a system of inscription they share. The dance grows in numbers, inviting further participants, as those who have been watching join the dance in a long line of shared movement. Even though some methods of inscription are enduring – choreographic features that give the dance its unique character – the dance is essentially participatory; its spatial formation is aimed at growing and including more participants. Spectators are not presumed to be passive spectators but rather bodies that become part of the dance. The moments in which the lawih breaks from the group allow him to change the rhythm and choreography, performing a sic-sensuous. This is an intervention of acts of writing creating a shared embodied space between two sensed bodies while allowing meaning to move from one body to another and to be negotiated in this process.

Van Aken describes the hierarchy as a lawih and a leading group that are meant to bring into the dance more participants, although roles may change and different people may occasionally comprise the leading group: 'in this collective frame, the body is the actor and the marker in micro-space; a complex variation of movements follows the steps proposed by the lawih that all the row should follow in an ordered and common way' (Aken 2006: 212). The space demarcated by the dabke, then, is organised choreographically so it can always expand, include more participators and allow for more people to join the conversation in movement.

The reading above, together with Van Aken's analysis and especially Rowe's political history of the dabke, shows that the dance has a distinct cultural history within Palestine and unique choreographic characteristics, its own system of inscription. Van Aken notes that the dabke remains a crucial site for local public expression and contestation by young refugees. At the same time, this clip reveals the sic-sensuous that dabke enables its participants to experience choreographically and politically. The dancers wear the Palestinian flag as part of their costume. This is a sharp and poignant reminder that this dance is not just about enlarging a community of shared bodies which arrange themselves according to the same logic and are inscribed in the same system of inscription, becoming equal in a shared space. This dance, as Van Aken notes, creates a shared space; but it also creates a shared space where that space is not allowed to exist according to international law.

The dabke provides a site that is local – it is grounded in the dancing bodies and in the spectator; but at the same time, due to its performance circumstances, celebrating a national identity that does not enjoy the protection of international law, it is also a global moment of interruption. The Palestinian sovereign state does not yet exist; at the same time it is very clear that the Palestinian people have a national dance that binds them together beyond difference. The dabke provides a language that binds people together against the backdrop of the legal and political realities that make the lives of Palestinian people unbearable. I hence read this as an exemplar of the way dance can be employed within the human rights doctrine.

On 12 July 2015, the anniversary of the Israeli attacks on Gaza, Palestinian activists organised a dabke flash mob in British sites of cultural and financial collaboration with Israel. The organisers said that they were keen to see how dabke dance could be used even more forcefully, critically and beautifully to stop business as usual (Glass 2015). Dabke flows from the bodies of Palestinian dancers to those who support them around the world; protesting together their modern statelessness. Moving from the reading of dance as a method of expressing human rights through sic-sensuous, I release towards the reality that hinders the Palestinian from achieving this legal and political recognition. The concluding part of this chapter will show how dance not only celebrates the ability of human beings to create their worlds when law and politics fail them, but also enables human beings to protest against wrongs done to them or other people within and without the human rights doctrine.

The affirmation of human rights through sic-sensuous releases from the bodies of dabke dancers, detained in checkpoints, to the body of Israeli choreographer Arkadi Zaides.

Arkadi Zaides's Archive: protest against human rights violations through dance

(www.youtube.com/watch?v=3hZW25c9Ulg)

Israeli choreographer Arkadi Zaides has created a substantial body of work on the Israel–Palestine conflict. Quiet (2009) involved Israeli and Arab dancers who shifted between scenes of anger and serenity; Land Research (2012) examines the relationship between man and land. However, in this part of the chapter I focus on Zaides's Archive, a work from 2014. According to Zaides's website:

> B'Tselem is the Israeli Information Centre for Human Rights in the Occupied Territories. In 2007 the organization initiated a project, in which video cameras are distributed to Palestinians living in high-conflict areas. The project aims to provide an ongoing documentation of human rights violations and to expose the reality of life under occupation to both the Israeli and international public.

In this work Arkadi Zaides deepens his artistic exploration of the ongoing conflict in Israel–Palestine. Work filmed by volunteers of the B'Tselem Camera Project is selected and reviewed. Zaides brings the viewers' attention to the bodies of Israelis, as they have been captured on camera, and to the physical reactions to which they resort in various confrontational situations. The Palestinians remain behind the camera. Nevertheless, their movement, voice and point of view are highly present, determining the spectator's perspective (Zaides 2014).

I focus upon the choreographic language of the work, which I have been calling the strong reading of political dance. The work powerfully and persuasively questions the concept of a spectator and an agent, separated by boundaries between two bodies. The footage used throughout this choreographic work is documented by Palestinians who carry cameras. Their bodies enable the creation of the archival material. Zaides is the Israeli spectator who mimics the movement of settlers and soldiers viewed on screen, sometimes violent, sometimes complacent. His body reacts to the screen, his movement embodies the motion of the Israeli structures as viewed by the Palestinian archivists. At the same time, the spectator, sitting in the auditorium, is spatially located in the embodied position of the Palestinian documenting the abuses shown.

Zaides emulates the motion of a soldier, shifting slowly, lurking; he mimics the motion of settlers throwing stones. Later he proceeds to mimic the actions of settlers chasing away sheep. The movement is repetitive. The spectator is always on the edge of their seat, never aware of what is coming next. That viewpoint, caught in never-ending suspension, belongs to the absent bodies of the Palestinian film-makers. The spectator is released into absent bodies.

Zaides's embodied language becomes one with his objects, the bodies he is emulating and transforming himself into. His body is released into the bodies that sustain the Occupation. Simultaneously in moments of rest and lack of movement, Zaides assumes the spatial position of the invisible archivist, the camera-based Palestinian. He is, through his embodied motion, negating the boundary between spectator and agent, wrongdoer and victim. He shows that our bodies are moulded by violence constituted by aggressive, volatile structures of power which make us complacent and stop us from asking questions about structures of domination that inhabit our lives. Zaides shows that lack of resistance is in itself partaking in human rights violations and enabling the sustaining structures of violence.

Reviews have celebrated this work by Zaides:

> Zaides is not saying anything about Israel's actions towards the Palestinians other than what the Israelis themselves are saying with their own bodies. The archival film that is the starting point of Archive is rough footage of transgressions by Israeli settlers and soldiers seen through the lens of cameras given to Palestinian citizens by the Israeli Human Rights Organisation B'Tselem for the express purpose of documenting them. Zaides is in turn looking at the corporal and vocal gestures of the aggressors and exploring the genesis of those same gestures – stone throwing, sheep scattering, olive branch destruction, verbal and physical intimidation, among others – in his own body. The result is visceral, poignant and disturbing to the point you wish it would stop. (Minns 2015)

Another review states: 'Zaides' energy is disturbingly neutral as he repeats this exercise. One does not get the sense that is he telling the audience how to interpret the material; rather, he lets the physical and vocal gestures speak for themselves, demanding that we position ourselves in relation to the images before us' (Simard 2015). Commenting on the end of the clip shown, in which Zaides emulates the vocality of the soldiers, another reviewer writes: 'Archive is at its most powerful near the end, when Zaides replicates the vocalisations of the men in the videos into a microphone, looping them, building a soundtrack that is increasingly oppressive and violent. It's hard to bear even for a few minutes. Imagine for hours, for weeks, for years ...' (Anonymous 2015; uncredited, available online). The piece is successful because it is unsettling. It allows spectators not only to see the world from occupied Palestine; it also allows the spectators to assume the embodied position of Palestinians.

We revisit here Isadora Duncan's moment of sic-sensuous in which she contested that which is beautiful and created a shared space of dialogue in that moment of rebellion. Zaides, too, works through challenging the conception of dance as creating an aesthetically pleasing experience; it is through the presentation of the ugly day-to-day lives of his absent Palestinian subjects that he inscribes his unique language of movement and creates a shared embodied space.

Zaides opens up a shared embodied space by enabling spectators to experience the transience between the body of the aggressor and the experience of the spectator of violence. For a short while, through the unique choreographic technique underlying this piece, the spectators who watch the piece share an embodied space with the Palestinians documenting human rights abuse. They become engraved in structures and languages of violence.

Archive transgresses the boundaries between aggressors and victims that allow structures of domination and violence to sustain themselves. The work shows that we all can be aggressors. At the same time it brings us closer in conversation with those who are subjected to violence and oppression, day in, day out. The work allows the spectators to feel that they are all victims of human rights violations and that those abuses benefit no one. It creates a moment of shared embodied space that enables the presentation of permeable boundaries between the self and other. I revisit Hannah Arendt's argument concerning the duality of presentation of difference and equality. It is the underlying human equality that allows the performance of difference. Archive also shows that the absent Palestinian documenters are equal to those spectators who assume their spatial position. The performance of sic-sensuous through this work, the presentation of those choreographic features that are not aesthetically pleasing, is politically powerful in its creation of a shared embodied space between two subjects who cannot come into dialogue in the world outside the theatre. They are separated by walls and checkpoints, structures of separation that do not allow sensed bodies to converse with each other. In this absence of conversation the realisation of the body stalled at the checkpoint is not being articulated to the body installing that checkpoint. The strong reading of political dance, the creation of an embodied shared space that transcends words, allows for that realisation of equality. Archive, in the most powerful way, allows the spectator to be inscribed with the languages that create the world of the people of Palestine. Zaides allows the Palestinians who have documented the footage to inscribe their human rights on the bodies of their spectators when other political structures inhibit this process from taking place.

The work received considerable attention from various organisations, and Zaides won an award from the Emile Zola Human Rights Cathedral. Moreover, the work was discussed beyond the world of dance audiences. In June 2015, shortly after the election of the majority Likud government in Israel, which signalled a further move to the right, newly elected Minister of Culture Miri Regev announced that she was going to remove the logo of Israel's Ministry of Culture from any merchandise promoting this choreographic work. This followed complaints from right-wing protesters. Regev had referred in the past to the work as 'a disgrace to the country' (Glick 2015). Once again the reader–spectator is reminded of Isadora Duncan's moment of offence in Boston in 1922. Sic-sensuous releases far from the formal space of the theatre in which it takes place. The resistance that Zaides shows, consequently, is far from being theoretical; it penetrated the political structures that it aimed at attacking. This is the quintessential moment of a clash between weak and strong readings of political dance. State structures become permeated through embodied dissent experienced by spectators of this dance performance. The Palestinians who have provided the documentation for the archives of the piece have indeed interrupted the Israeli government. That moment of interruption occurred through the shared embodied space they inhabited with the Israeli spectators that were unsettled by watching this piece. Revisiting Martha Graham's famous quotation, we see that the body not only says what words cannot, it challenges and questions the boundaries posed by words. Consequently, reading human rights as enacted through dance is universal in its emphasis on the ability to unsettle; to interrupt; to insert different languages into symbolic webs of meaning. The body is able to interrupt universally; in this case it is the absent body that interrupts and creates sensation. This reading of human rights through dance is always local, grounded in a unique embodied dialogue between the spectator's body filling the void in this choreographic work and Zaides's repetition of archived movement onstage. Checkpoints and walls may cause some bodies to be absent from demarcated political spaces; but dance can transcend those boundaries and make those bodies very present and able to claim their own human rights.

Conclusions: a danced conception of human rights

Bodies contracting into themselves and releasing into shared communities can move boundaries that are not just choreographic. Those bodies can transcend legal-political boundaries that other political webs of signification sustain. Dabke dance released from the bodies of its dancers, in the West Bank and Jordan Valley, into a shared embodied space; that space in turn was released further into a flash mob supporting the Palestinian struggle for sovereignty. At the same time, those bodies, stalled at checkpoints and put behind walls, are released into the bodies of the spectators of Arkadi Zaides's *Archive*. Those moments of release confirmed that all sensuous bodies sharing a space are equal, and yet distinct; they require a robust legal-political framework that protects them from abuse and degradation. They require human rights.

In both these cases dance allows for the assertion of the ability to use the body as a powerful mechanism of inscription, affirming the equality of the body inscribing upon the body. The use of dance and the focus on spectatorship in both case studies, in very different ways, allows for discussion of human rights and their abuses without consolidating the categories of victims. Both readings move to an interpretation of human rights through sic-sensuous and rights claims being made by the subjects themselves. In the case of dabke, the bodies of dancers and spectators contributed to its perception as a national dance for a country striving for sovereignty that would allow its subjects to make human rights claims. In the case of *Archive*, dance created a unique choreographic setting that allowed the audience to share embodied space with the Palestinians who documented human rights abuses.

The strong reading of political dance shifts our focus towards the use of choreographic elements to create a shared space between various participants in both those instances of dance. That shared space transcends the lack of shared spaces constituted by formal political and legal mechanisms (which in turn hinder the possibility for human rights claims to be made by Palestinians). Dance creates a world in which Palestinian subjects are affirmed as equal to Israelis; in which the bodies of both sides command equal respect and are treated as equally dignified.

The dancers dancing their human rights in this chapter make their human rights claims through motion. This inscription pushes for a reinterpretation of the ontology and epistemology of the argument. The readings of both the dances discussed present the possibility of building a world through movement. The world is never stable, never confined to a specific space; it is constantly re-enacted by the interlocutors in the embodied conversation. The ontological vulnerability of human rights as being part of two worlds in one becomes part of the epistemology of human rights subjects, constantly enacting that new world in which they are equal subjects through their bodies. Indeed, for some subjects of the human rights doctrine the current political world offers few solutions for their legal vulnerability. Through dance they mobilise ways of knowing and show that they are never vulnerable; no one needs to act on their behalf. I argue that dance allows for an interpretation of human rights in movement, in a world that is constantly becoming.

In this chapter I have argued that dance can be mobilised to transcend obstacles that the human rights doctrine faces in our contemporary world. The doctrine of human rights still requires local mechanisms for rights claims to be made, though they always appeal to the universal. My analysis is always focused on the most local unit of claiming human rights, the human body. At the same time, the use of dance transcends that unit and is able to articulate messages intertwined in the ethos of human rights as a recognition of inherent dignity and inalienable rights. There is no positing of one group of people as victims and they are actively and powerfully reconfiguring their shared lives and shaping the way they would like their rights to be claimed. This reading allows us to bring the discussion of human rights back to the human body and away from transcendental conceptions of the human, disengaged from the local experiences of those who shape and claim human rights. The concept of sic-sensuous as always inscribing from the sensed body means that the subject always claims their rights from a definite space, their own body, and in their own language.

Consequently, we release towards a new conceptualisation of human rights through dance. Dance, we have seen, allows for further participation in debates around human rights in methods that transcend some of the obstacles towards further implementation of the doctrine. It allows for the local moment of claiming human rights – or violation of human rights – to be communicated beyond power structures that oppose the doctrine. This reading gives both the affirmation of human rights and resistance towards their violation a new kind of language. The body is able to transcend structures of domination that hinder it from feeling compassion towards the body of the Other. The moving body relates to the moved body, whether or not political-legal structures are in place to enable this relationship and sustain this relationality. Those moments of shared empathy enable the recognition *through the body* of the underlying assumption of the human rights doctrine: *that all human beings are equal in dignity.* This affirmation allows the reader–spectator to progress towards the last act in this argument: its conclusions.

Note

1   Rowe is married to a Palestinian dancer and his study draws on his experiences teaching dance in Palestine as well as in-depth interviews with dance practitioners in Palestine.

Conclusions: the dancer of the future dancing radical hope

Dance plays a crucial role in Jonathan Lear's seminal work on the Native American tribe, the Crow peoples, and their gains and losses in their attempt to sustain communal life under white conquest. Lear pays much attention to the sun dance, a prayer for revenge which lapsed around 1875 and was relearned around 1941, from the Crow's enemies, the Shoshone tribe (Lear 2008). The sun dance was central to the Crow form of life, and intimately related to various other elements of their culture, specifically warfare. Lear asks:

> What is one to do with the sun dance when it is no longer possible to fight? Roughly speaking, a culture faced with this kind of devastation has three choices:
>
> 1. Keep dancing even though the point of the dance has been lost. The ritual continues, though no one can any longer say what the dance is for.
> 2. Invent a new aim for the dance. The dance continues, but its purpose is, for example, to facilitate good negotiations with whites, usher good weather for farming, or restore health to a sick relative.
> 3. Give up the dance. This is an implicit recognition that there is no longer any point in dancing the sun dance. (Lear 2008: 36)

Lear argues that the sun dance, after the Crow's traditional way of life had ceased, cannot be danced; its steps could be repeated but the system of signification that gave it its meaning had been lost. Lear argues that 'concepts get their lives through the lives we are able to live with them' (Lear 2008: 37); further, 'circumstances are such that there is no practical possibility of our performing those acts, or the very acts themselves have ceased to make sense' (Lear 2008: 38). At the conclusion of the book Lear asks: 'is this a maintenance of re-introduction of a tradition – or is the name of "tradition" being invoked to invent new rituals?' He goes on to offer a partial answer: 'it is not for me to answer this question: that is and will be the task of Crow poets, of Crow leaders and their followers' (Lear 2008: 152). When this statement is read together with option no. 2 and the core argument of this book, we may find another possibility for the sun dance, one for which traces can be found in Lear's argument. Further, we are reminded of Martha Graham's statement, quoted in Chapter 3, according to which it is not for her to understand the meaning of her dance. That possibility is the creation of a conceptual symbolic system that cannot be articulated in words, cannot be signified in existing concepts, but creates a world through the dance itself.

Bonnie Honig critiques Lear's insistence on ethics rather than politics. A move to a focus on politics, she argues, can shed light on the ability to question power and on concepts of inequality and resistance (Honig 2015). In addition, Honig critiques Lear's admiration for the singular leader rather than for action-in-concert. She writes: 'hope insists on the importance of the held hands and not on the courage of a radical individual with radical hope' (Honig 2015: 33). In a response to Honig's essay, Jason Frank asks us to revisit what Tocqueville sees as 'the political itself', the capacity of ordinary people to respond collectively to challenges they commonly face' (Frank 2015: 638). James Martel also critiques the insistence on teleology and the singular leader and the avoidance of politics as action 'on our own' (Martel 2015). I revisit here one of my core methodological assumptions, which, in an argument focusing on inscription, is far more than an underlying method. The interpretation of politics as arising from collective action that always transcends the individual and yet starts from one moving body can be found in Eleanor Marx's essay 'The Woman Question from a Socialist Point of View' (Marx 1886) in which the categories of action used are woman and man; always beyond the individual but starting from Eleanor's own inscription upon history. Further, I draw my use of this text from the powerful reading of this argument in context in Rachel Holmes's groundbreaking biography where the use of those categories is intimately related to Eleanor's understanding of history; in which beyond the dialectical view presented by her father she sees her intervention as the next stage as 'the sequel' (Holmes 2014: 449). Eleanor Marx (known as 'Tussy') provides us with what these radical democratic critiques of Lear's virtue ethics seek: a category of action that in its very becoming unfolds a new future while always being grounded in a collective.

What if, with Martel's, Frank's and Honig's appeal to move away from the singular leader towards the people; what if we follow Tussy and go back to investigate action together, and bring back equality, and start listening to the sun dancers themselves? What if, with Lear's own question, and with Honig's critique of Lear, we don't ask the poets to narrate the new meaning inserted into the sun dance? What if we do not seek the Crow poet to explain the meaning that is or is not within the dance, but rather ask the dancers who have been practising it, through its turbulent history, without seeing their actions as secondary to those who narrate them? What if we use this tension to revisit Arendt's juxtaposition of equality and difference, and assume that it is because we are equal that we can speak to each other, in words or movement (but it is because we are different that we want to speak to each other and express that natality)? What if we let Tussy invite us into the sequel, a world in which lives collide more and further equality is claimed? A new way of investigating the sun dance emerges. This interpretation has been written upon the argument of this book by its dancing interlocutors: the argument of relational movement which creates an independent world, performing a uniquely danced voice but arising out of embodied equality.

A documentary book and film on Crow and the sun dance offer us a snapshot of this ritual in the actions and movements of its interlocutors. Written by Thomas Yellowtail, with contributions from various Crow elders, both book and film offer an insight into this complex ceremony that is practised over several days. James Trosper, a Shoshone/Arpaho elder, writes: 'in the sundance we pray for the tribe, we pray for our country. Those prayers are really offered for all Indian people, for the whole world' (Yellowtail 2007: 91).

Even in its short trailer (www.youtube.com/watch?v=LQrW-3BZtyQ) we see some of the characteristics of dance discussed throughout this book: the sun dance was always relational, never practised alone; it has its own method of inscription, its own form of conduct known only by its practitioners. The old Crow world is lost; but it may be that by repeating the sun dance they will slowly build their new world, which creates a sic-sensuous in its conditions of arising and in its language; learned from their enemies, in the face of cultural devastation, the sun dance renews itself and provides new spaces for generating shared meaning out of re- and misinterpretations. The sun dance releases from the body of the individual dancer, towards dancing with them in the specific time-place in which it is performed. It may be that the steps were relearned by copying the Shoshone, but by rearticulating them and bringing them into new spaces with new participants the Crow are creating a new world. Alternative spaces of dissent for the people of the Crow are unravelled by the sun dance; and its new meaning is created by them, equally contributing to the dance. But the sun dance goes one step further; it releases from that dancing community towards a world in which it will one day make sense. The dance is performed in a world not yet built; a world in which Crow culture once again is constitutive for their way of life, and in which they can dance the sundance both to inscribe events that accompanied its long and turbulent history but also to unravel a new future. The Crow people dance radical hope. The sun dancers are dancers in a world not yet built.

The sun dance creates its own system of signification that may well not be easily articulated in words and retold as a story, and histories, as well as narratives of cultural oppression and disenfranchisement, are now constitutive of its system of inscription. It starts from a singular contracting body, expressing its uniqueness, and releasing into other bodies responding to it. The world constructed by the dance is never the world of solitary, courageous leaders acting on their own; the dance is relational in and of itself, never practised alone. I read in the example of the sun dance another tension between the strong and weak reading of political dance; only here it is stated that the weak reading no longer exists. There are no words available to describe this dance. This does not stop the reader–spectator from seeking the strong reading of political dance – politics articulated within dance itself, and allowing for a world of signification to unravel through movement.

Honig reads the tribal elders of the Crow as the Greek chorus (Honig 2015). The sundance allows for a reading of a different kind of chorus; a shared space including elders and youngers, spectators and dancers. The chorus of the sun dance tells the story of cultural catastrophe but also the story of radical hope. This chorus unravels a world to be built in the steps of the dancers and engrained on their bodies. This allows us to revisit the woman who wanted to dance the chorus, Isadora Duncan.

Isadora Duncan wrote to her adopted daughter, Irma Duncan, asking about her hopes for the summer of 1925, and expressing an interest in visiting Jerusalem (Duncan 1929: 314). Duncan never made it to Jerusalem. Looking at the argument of Chapter 6 of this book it is hard to imagine that Isadora Duncan would have enjoyed her visit to contemporary Jerusalem; Jerusalem whose space is fractured by checkpoints and separation walls. And yet Duncan allows us to bring some radical hope into the conclusion of this argument. The reader–spectator is reminded that in The Dance of the Future Duncan writes about the dancer of the future, the free spirit inhabiting the body of new woman (Duncan 1994). Further, let us revisit the third dancer, larger than all humanity itself. Duncan's dancer of the future, or the third dancer, enables us to imagine a humanity not yet here. Duncan's dancers of the future – leading to further interruptions, and conceptually enabling us to read many other dancers of the future, from South Africa to Palestine, through protests against gendered violence – not only protest the worlds in which they are deemed unequal; in their intervention they dance in a world not yet built. In that world, their bodies are perceived as equal to those who oppress them; through their dance they show that we are all equal as embodied beings and deserve to be treated with respect and dignity. Moments of sic-sensuous are crucial here, as they not only unravel different forms of meaning through aesthetic and political interventions; they unravel a world in which those meanings will make sense. The dancer of the future, arriving in Jerusalem, unravels a world in which there is equal respect for human rights, dignity and equality of all; a world in which human beings can express joy and pain through their bodies with no fear of oppression or of the silencing of their voices. The dancer of the future brings with her a new interpretation of humanity through dance.

The performance of the argument nearly draws to a close and it is time to summon the interlocutors of this book for their curtain call. From Isadora Duncan, who wanted to dance the chorus, and proved that she was always red, regardless of what she said or wore; through Martha Graham, whose psyche was divided between herself and her chorus, and in turn allowed uninvited audience members to perform their equality, the argument danced equality, solidarity and intervention. It then proceeded to the long line of gumboot dancers, who released in a language they were not entitled to speak, and in this way created a space for themselves, a world in which they were to make sense before it was even built. The argument moves to global responses to Eve Ensler's call for the utilisation of dance against violence, those responses subverting intention at times but creating different spaces in which bodies could meet and heal together. The dance continues through the dabke, allowing for people to join and create a shared embodied symbolic space where international law cannot allow that to be created. The argument then creates an embodied dialogue between the dabke dancers, stalled in checkpoints, and Arkadi Zaides's unravelling of a space for a chorus of Palestinian narrators, made absent by systematic infringement upon their human rights. The argument dances equality and solidarity; dignity and respect. At the same time it allows the less glorious parts of our political lives to be performed and elaborated, in a world that sometimes does not allow those elements to be put forth in words.

Dance releases from one body in motion to the embodied space it unravels. That embodied space has its own unique system of inscription. This world simultaneously changes the ontological position of the dancer: it changes their body; and at the same time it creates a break in epistemology: it introduces radically new ways of knowing and seeing the world within and without the dance. Dance then allows for the creation of an ontology of a subject in becoming, constituting itself through this process of inscription. Reading dance as a world allows for a wide point of view encompassing various angles of dancers' lives. Some of those points of view have penetrated and tainted other worlds in which those dancers live. Some of those worlds are yet to be unravelled. But the movement of the dance is propelled by hope, and at times radical hope, which has pushed dancers to never stand still even when their experience of humanity had failed them.

This book has provided two larger, conceptual gestures. The first gesture shifts the reader–spectator to question what they read as politics. Politics cannot and should not be reduced to words. People have always danced about politics. In fact, I have argued, people have danced politics in manifold ways. They have created political worlds that at times transcended verbal language. In those worlds dance has enabled both sharing and subversion; both relationality and distinction.

The second gesture pushes the reader–spectator to rethink what is assumed to be dance. I have interpreted dance throughout the book in the widest possible sense, from perhaps the two most iconic names of modern dance in the twentieth century to grassroots practices far from the West. Moreover, deconstructing the dances through close readings has demonstrated that every dance has its own system of inscription, an embodied language unique to that form of dance and to its world. Graham's contraction, the dabke stomping, Duncan's use of the solar plexus, gumboot dance's interplay between singles and unison and Arkadi Zaides's use of the absent dancers as a focal point: all have a unique choreographic logic that makes sense within their world. Ensler's attempt to create a global danced system of inscription created multiple global responses. Human beings have been making sense to themselves through their bodies for a very long time. Every so often, those systems of inscription make sense beyond the danced world and unravel wrongs in other political worlds too. Contracting into a singular body releases a possibility for multiple systems of signification; at times, those systems of signification create worlds that do not make sense yet, but they may do so through multiple dancers of the future.

Every day, numerous people around the world dance. They contract into their embodied selves, investigating their corporeal possibilities, inscribing upon themselves in manifold systems of inscription. At the same time, their bodies release to others, creating dialogues in motion, between two bodies which always live in multiple systems of signification, some translatable into the spoken word, some not. Every day, subjects create embodied worlds through sweat and tears, joy and pain; they bring their life stories into embodied communication. Through moments of sic-sensuous, in which these dancers challenge what is a politically and aesthetically legible articulation, they release into new worlds that they at times know not themselves. These worlds can bring new possibilities for a life together of respect towards the equality of all human bodies.

Dance is a way to dissent from politics practised in words. It is a way to reclaim spaces where those are not always granted; it is a way to investigate a world experienced by a single embodied subject and in its relationship to others. It allows for systems of inscription to bring it into being as manifold embodied languages; in so doing, it allows its subjects to occupy spaces not always available to them otherwise.

What we, as readers–spectators, must do, is hone our viewing and listening, and be attentive to those embodied voices that otherwise may get lost; bring into our discourse those corporeal dialogues that occur every day and everywhere between human beings. This book has shown that dance opens up a vista for a different kind of political intervention; one which creates a clash between movement and words, bodies and verbal language. We must, then, allow for those voices to be registered not only within a phenomenological independent world operating within its own set of rules but as one that is able to rupture other forms of politics.

Dance moves human beings beyond boundaries – of their own bodies, constantly reinterpreted and reconfigured as spaces; and of their shared worlds, challenging the limits of who they may speak with and who perceives them as equal interlocutors.

At the same time, dance is not all radical hope; indeed, it brings with it some of the illnesses and challenges that other forms of politics bring to human lives; it does not always allow for equality in dignity or respect; but it does allow for tears in the shared sensed fabric in which those deemed unequal carve for themselves a space of their own. The strong reading of political dance allows us to listen to those who often may go unnoticed in other systems of signification, and by so doing to create greater equality in our own political discourse. From the discourse around the two world wars and the Cold War discussed in the reading of Duncan and Graham, to racial inequality in South Africa, to gender violence and to human rights abuses, let us invite more interlocutors about this into our political conversation. We must be attentive to moments in which human beings around the world claim spaces for their bodies and their danced voices; in which they allow dance to move them beyond boundaries. Let us allow ourselves to be moved too.

References

AGAMBEN, G. (1998). *Homo Sacer: Sovereign Power and Bare Life*. Stanford, CA, Stanford University Press.

AKEN, M. V. (2006). 'Dancing belonging: contesting dabkeh in the Jordan Valley, Jordan.' *Journal of Ethnic and Migration Studies* 32(2): 203–22.

ANONYMOUS (1967). *Martha Graham playbill*: Saville Theatre, London.

—— (2015). 'Archive: a review.' Retrieved 10.7.2016 from http://www.localgestures.com/dance/archive-a-review.

ARENDT, H. (1976). *The Origins of Totalitarianism*. Orlando, Harcourt Books.

—— (1998). *The Human Condition*. Chicago, IL, University of Chicago Press.

ARMITAGE, M. (1966). *Martha Graham*. New York, Dance Horizons.

AZOULAY, A. (2015). 'What are human rights?' *Comparative Studies of South Asia, Africa and the Middle East* 35(1): 8–20.

BALIBAR, E. (2007). '(De)constructing the human as human institution: a reflection on the coherence of Hannah Arendt's practical philosophy.' *Social Research* 74(3): 727–38.

BANNERMAN, H. (1999). 'An overview of the development of Martha Graham's movement system (1926–1991).' *Dance Research* 17(2): 9–46.

—— (2010). 'Ancient myths and modern moves: the Greek-inspired dance-theatre of Martha Graham.' *The Ancient Dancer in the Modern World*, ed. F. MACINTOSH. Oxford, Oxford University Press, pp. 255–77.

BENHABIB, S. (2006). *Another Cosmopolitanism*. Oxford, Oxford University Press.

BOSTEELS, B. (2003). 'Nonplaces: an anecdoted topography of contemporary French theory.' *Diacritics* 33(3/4): 117–39.

BRANCHINIA, C. et al. (2013). '"One Billion Rising" at Johns Hopkins Bloomberg School of Public Health: a reflection.' *Reproductive Health Matters* 21(41): 251–3.

BRECKENRIDGE, K. (1998). '"We must speak for ourselves": the rise and fall of a public sphere on the South African gold mines, 1920 to 1931.' *Comparative Studies in Society and History* 40(1): 71–108.

BURT, R. (1998). 'Dance, gender and psychoanalysis: Martha Graham's "Night Journey".' *Dance Research Journal* 30(1): 34–53.

CHAMBERS, C. (2006). *Here We Stand: Politics, Performers and Performance*. London, Nick Hern.

COPELAND, R. (2004). *Merce Cunningham and the Modernizing of Modern Dance*. New York and London, Routledge.

CROFT, C. (2015). *Dancers as Diplomats: American Choreography in Cultural Exchange*. Oxford, Oxford University Press.

DALY, A. (1992). 'Dance history and feminist theory: reconsidering Isadora Duncan and the male gaze.' *Gender and Performance: The Presentation of Difference in the Performing Arts*, ed. L. SENELICK. Hanover, NH, Tufts University/University Press of New England: pp. 230–55.

—— (1995). *Done into Dance: Isadora Duncan in America*. Middletown, CT, Wesleyan University Press.

DENBY, E. (1986). *Dance Writings*. New York, Knopf.

DIKEC, M. (2005). 'Space, politics and the political.' *Environment and Planning D: Society and Space* 23: 171–88.

DIXON, N. (1998). 'Behind the "gumboot dance".' Retrieved 20.4.2015 from www.greenleft.org.au/node/16224.

DUNCAN, I. (1929). *Isadora Duncan's Russian Days and her Last Years in France*. London, Victor Gollancz.

—— (1970). *The Technique of Isadora Duncan*. New York, Dance Horizons.

DUNCAN, I. (1977). *The Art of the Dance*. New York, Theatre Arts Books.

—— (1994). *Isadora Speaks: Writings and Speeches of Isadora Duncan*. Chicago, IL, Charles H. Kerr Publishing Company.

—— (1995). *My Life*. New York and London, Liveright.

ELIOT, T. S. (1959) *Four Quartets*. London : Faber and Faber.

ENSLER, E. (2013a). *In the Body of the World: A Memoir of Cancer and Connection*. New York, Picador.

—— (2013b). 'We have an anthem.' Retrieved 8.7.2016 from http://2013.onebillionrising.org/blog/we-have-an-anthem.

FARGION, J. T. (1998). 'The gumboot dance: sell-out or symbol?' Retrieved 21.4.2015 from www.doc4net.com/doc/3800730596346.

FOSTER, S. (2011). *Choreographing Empathy: Kinesthesia in Performance*. London, Routledge.

FOSTER, S. L. (1995). 'Choreographing history.' *Choreographing History*, ed. S. L. FOSTER. Bloomington, IN, Indiana University Press: pp. 3–25.

FRANK, J. (2015). 'Collective actors, common desires.' *Political Research Quarterly* 68(3): 637–41.

FRANKO, M. (1995). *Dancing Modernism/Performing Politics*. Bloomington, IN, Indiana University Press.

—— (2011). 'Archeological choreographic practices: Foucault and Forsythe.' *History of the Human Sciences* 24(4): 97–112.

—— (2012). *Martha Graham in Love and War: The Life in the Work*. New York, Oxford University Press.

FRASER, N. (1990). 'Rethinking the public sphere: a contribution to the critique of actually existing democracy.' *social text* 1(25–6): 56–80.

FUCHS, A. (2002). *Playing the Market: The Market Theatre, Johannesburg.* Amsterdam, Rodopi.

GILBERT, H. (2001). *Postcolonial Plays: An Anthology.* London and New York, Routledge.

GLASS, D. (2015). 'Dabke dancing to tell another narrative.' Retrieved 20.7.2015 from www.redpepper.org.uk/dabke-dancing-to-tell-another-narrative/.

GLICK, S. (2015). 'Symbol of the Ministry of Culture removed from a show inspired by "Betselem".' Retrieved 27.6.2015 from www.ynet.co.il/articles/0,7340,L-4663643,00.html.

GOLD, S. (1984). *A Selection of Isadora Duncan Dances: The Schubert Selection.* Newport Beach, CA, Sutton Movement Writing Press.

GORMLEY, A. et al. (2008). 'Public space and the body.' *Subjectivity* 24: 356–75.

GRAFF, E. (1997). *Stepping Left: Dance and Politics in New York City, 1928–1942.* Durham and London, Duke University Press.

GRAHAM, M. (1937). 'Martha Graham 1937.' *The Visions of Modern Dance in the Words of its Creators*, eds. J. M. BROWN, N. MINDLIN and C. H. WOODFORD. London, Dance Books, pp. 50–3.

—— (1973). *The Martha Graham Notebooks.* New York, Harcourt Brace Jovanovich Inc.

GREEN, J. (2002–3). 'Foucault and the training of docile bodies.' *Arts and learning research journal* 19(1): 99–126.

GÜNDOĞDU, A. (2015). *Rightlessness in an Age of Rights: Hannah Arendt and the Contemporary Struggles of Migrants.* Oxford, Oxford University Press.

HALPERN, A. J. (1991). *The Technique of Martha Graham.* Pennington, NJ, Society of Dance Scholars at Princeton Periodicals.

HOLMES, R. (2014). *Eleanor Marx: A Life.* London, Bloomsbury.

HONIG, B. (2013). *Antigone, Interrupted.* Cambridge, Cambridge University Press.

—— (2015). 'Public things: Jonathan Lear's Radical Hope, Lars Von Trier's Melancholia, and the democratic need.' *Political Research Quarterly* 68(3): 623–36.

HOROSKO, M. (2002). *Martha Graham: The Evolution of Her Dance Theory and Training.* Gainsville, Fl, University of Florida Press.

INGRAM, J. D. (2008). 'What is a "right to have rights"? Three images of the politics of human rights.' *American political science review* 102(4): 402–16.

JONES, S. (2009). '"At the still point of time": T. S. Eliot, dance,and modernism.' *Dance Research Journal* 41(2): 31–51.

—— (2013). *Literature, Modernism and Dance.* Oxford, Oxford University Press.

KOLB, A. (2011). *Dance and Politics.* Bern and Oxford, Peter Lang.

KURTH, P. (2002). *Isadora: A Sensational Life.* London, Little, Brown.

LAMOTHE, K. L. (2006). *Nietzsche's Dancers: Isadora Duncan, Martha Graham and the Revaluation of Christian Values.* New York, Basingstoke, Palgrave McMillan.

LEAR, J. (2008). *Radical Hope: Ethics in the Face of Cultural Devastation.* Cambridge, MA and London, Harvard University Press.

LEPECKI, A. (2006). *Exhausting Dance: Performance and the Politics of Movement.* London, Routledge.

LEVIEN, J. (1994). *Duncan Dance: A Guide for Young People Ages Six to Sixteen.* New Jersey, NJ, Princeton Book Company.

LOOTS, L. (1997). 'Re-remembering protest theater in South Africa.' *Critical Arts: South–North Cultural and Media Studies* 11(1–2): 142–52.

MANNING, E. (2007). *Politics of Touch: Sense, Movement, Sovereignty.* Minneapolis, MN and London, University of Minnesota Press.

MAPONYA, M. (1995). *Doing Plays for a Change: Five Works.* Johannesburg, Witwatersrand University Press.

MARTEL, J. (2015). 'Against thinning and teleology: politics and objects in the face of catastrophe in Lear and Von Terrier.' *Political Research Quarterly* 68(3): 642–6.

MARTIN, R. (1998). *Critical Moves: Dance Studies in Theory and Politics.* Durham and London, Duke University Press.

MARX, E. (1886). 'The Woman Question from a Socialist Point of View.' Retrieved 10.7.2016 from https://www.marxists.org/archive/eleanor-marx/works/womanq.htm.

McDONAGH, D. (1974). *Martha Graham: A Biography.* Newton Abbot UK, David & Charles.

McNAY, L. (2014). *The Misguided Search for the Political.* Cambridge, Polity Press.

MINNS, N. (2015). 'Arkadi Zaides: Archive.' Retrieved 25.6.2015 from http://writingaboutdance.com/performance/arkadi-zaides-archive/.

MULLER, C. A. (2008). *Focus: Music of South Africa.* New York, Routledge.

MULLER, C. and J. T. FARGION (1999). 'Bhaca migrants, and Fred Astaire: South African worker dance and musical style.' *African Music* 7(4): 88–109.

NAHUMCK, N. C. (1994). *Isadora Duncan: The Dances.* Washington, DC, National Museum of Women in Arts.

NIBBELINK, L. G. (2012). 'Radical intimacy: Ontroerend Goed meets the emancipated spectator.' *Contemporary Theatre Review*: 412–20.

NOLAND, C. (2009). *Agency and Embodiment: Performing Gesture/Producing Culture.* Cambridge and London, Harvard University Press.

OBR (2013). 'About One Billion Rising.' Retrieved from sundance.onebillionrising.org/about/campaign/one-billion-rising/.

OZGUBULUT, M. (2012). 'Introduction to the interactive learning environment of body music.' *Procedia – Social and Behavioral Sciences* 47: 751–5.

PAIN, R. (1991). 'Space, sexual violence and social control: interrogating geographical and feminist analysis of women's fear of crime.' *Progress in human geography* 15: 415–31.

PREVOTS, N. (2001). *Dance for Export: Cultural Diplomacy and the Cold War.* Middletown, CT, Wesleyan University Press.

RANCIÈRE, J. (2009). *The Politics of Aesthetics.* London and New York, Continuum.

—— (2010). *Dissensus: On Politics and Aesthetics*. London, Continuum.

REYNOLDS, D. and M. REASON (2012). *Kinesthetic Empathy in Creative and Cultural Practices*. Bristol, Intellect.

ROSE, G. (1999). 'Women and everyday spaces.' *Feminist Theory and the Body*, eds. J. P. and M. SHILDRICK. Edinburgh, Edinburgh University Press, pp. 359–71.

ROWE, N. (2010). *Raising Dust: A Cultural History of Dance in Palestine*. London, Tauris.

SCHNEIDER, I. (1968). *Isadora Duncan: The Russian Years*. London, Macdonald and Co.

SHAPIRO-PHIM, N. J. T. (2008). 'Introduction.' *Dance, Human Rights and Social Justice*, eds. N. JACKSON and T. SHAPIRO-PHIM. Lyham, MA, Toronto and Plymouth, The Scarecrow Press Inc, pp. xi–xxxiii.

SIMARD, H. (2015). 'Embodied aggression on screen and on stage: a review of Archive by Arkadi Zaides.' Retrieved 24.6.2015 from www.danscussions.com/2015/05/embodied aggression-on-screen-and-on.html?m=1.

STEADMAN, I. (1995). 'Introduction.' *Doing Plays for a Change: Five Works*, ed. M. MAPONYA. Johannesburg, Witwatersrand University Press, pp. 3–24.

STERN, S. J. and S. STRAUS (2014). 'Embracing paradox: human rights in the global age.' *The Human Rights Paradox: Universality and its Discontents*, eds. S. J. STERN and S. STRAUS. Madison, WI, University of Wisconsin Press, pp. 3–31.

SWYNGEDOUW, E. (2011). 'Interrogating post-democratization: reclaiming egalitarian political space.' *Political geography* 30: 370–80.

TERRY, W. (1960a). 'In perspective.' *Dance perspectives: the legacy of Isadora Duncan and Ruth St. Denis* 5(winter): 3–24.

—— (1960b). 'The witnesses.' *Dance perspectives: the legacy of Isadora Duncan and Ruth St. Denis* 5(winter): 25–54.

THOMAS, H. (1995). *Dance, Modernity and Culture: Explorations in the Sociology of Dance*. London and New York, Routledge.

THOMS, V. (2013). *Martha Graham: Gender and the Haunting of a Dance Pioneer*. Bristol, Intellect.

TSING, A. L. (2005). *Friction: An Ethnography of Global Connection*. London and New Jersey, NJ, Princeton University Press.

WOOD, M. T. (2012). 'Celebrating the anti-heroine: championing the fatal flaw in Martha Graham's female protagonists.' Retrieved 30.7.2012 from http://marthagraham.org/wp-content/uploads/2012/02/Martha-Graham-Celebrating-Anti-Heroine.pdf.

YELLOWTAIL, T. (2007). *Native Spirit: The Sun Dance Way*. Bloomington, IN, World Wisdom.

ZAIDES, A. (2014). 'Arkadi Zaides' Archive.' Retrieved 20.6.2015 from www.arkadizaides.com/archive.

Index